The

Moths of

Butterfly

Ridge

A Beginners Guide to Attracting and Identifying Moths in Ohio

2nd Edition

Christopher Kline

Butterfly Ridge Butterfly Conservation Center ltd.
17864 State Route 374
Rockbridge, Ohio 43149
www.butterfly-ridge.com

ISBN-13: 978-1734619713

Table of Contents

How to Use This Book   1

About Moths   4

Attracting Moths   10

Moths as Pollinators   12

What are Micromoths?   14

Moth Myths   15

Quick Reference to Moth Families   17

Moth Plates and Descriptions   22

Index   326

Thank you to all of our visitors to Butterfly Ridge's Saturday Night Lights programs, showing your enthusiasm and concern for these wonderful insects. Also thank you to the late Ira Kline for his willingness to stay up until the wee hours of the morning looking at moths with me. Finally thanks to Dr. Bruce Walsh of the University of Arizona for introducing me to the wonderful world of moths.

How To Use This Book

This book is designed to introduce the reader to the moths found in Ohio. Each moth species that has been identified at Butterfly Ridge Butterfly Conservation Center in southeast Ohio has been given a picture and a description. Within each description is a listing of common host plants for the moth species as well as tips to aid in the identification of each species.

In addition, for each species listed there is a timeline presented. The timeline represents the months March - November. The blue bar on the timeline represents the actually timeframe that the moth has been observed at Butterfly Ridge. The red bar represents the timeframe that the moth would be expected to be present at Butterfly Ridge based on data posted to BugGuide.net and the Moth Photographers Group at Mississippi State University.

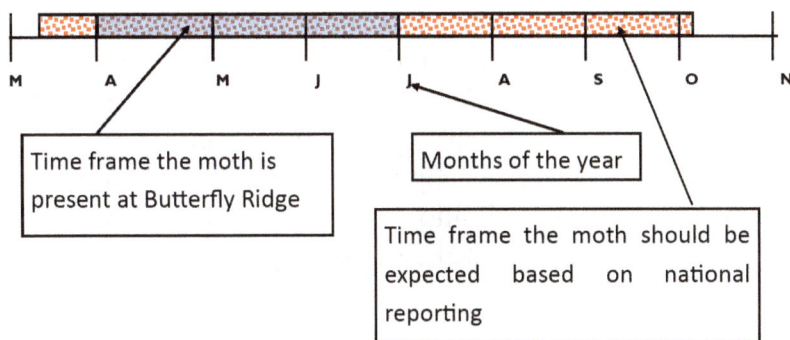

M   A   M   J   J   A   S   O   N

Time frame the moth is present at Butterfly Ridge

Months of the year

Time frame the moth should be expected based on national reporting

The descriptions for the moths will make more sense if you study the "About Moths" section of the book. This section will discuss the anatomy of the moth, including the names given to certain wing structures mentioned in the descriptions.

Colored arrows have been used in the book to emphasize certain identification features. The colors used for those arrows vary, and generally are chosen to make finding the arrows and structures easier.

Hodges Numbers
Each species of butterfly and moth is assigned a Hodges Number, based on the family and sub-family of each species. While the Hodges Number for a butterfly is rarely referenced, Hodges Numbers for moths are frequently used to help organize and discuss moths. The species represented in this book are arranged according to the Hodges Numbers for each species.

In addition, a colored bar is shown at the top of each photo page to represent different families and sub-families. For example, a purple bar is at the top of each page for the Saturnidae (Giant Silkmoth) moths. Once you begin to recognize moths by their family, the colored bars will allow you to quickly turn to the appropriate section of the book.

While the number of species observed at Butterfly Ridge numbers around 500 as of January, 2020, the number of moths that call southeast Ohio home is certainly far greater. Estimates for the number of moth species native to Hocking County, Ohio approach 1,500!

While this book will be periodically updated, it will never contain 1,500 species. That book would be far to large and cumbersome to be useful. The moths that you will find in this book are mostly large, with distinctive features to help the beginning moth-er become more familiar with moths and their identification. However, in this 2nd edition more of the micro-moths have been included showing that great beauty can come in small packages!

About Moths

Moths and butterflies are both in the insect order Lepidoptera. There are some keys differences between moths and butterflies. These are shown in the chart below and in the figures that follow. Keep in mind, there are exceptions for many of the rules that follow.

<u>Characteristic</u>	<u>Moth</u>	<u>Butterfly</u>
Active period	Nocturnal (night)	Diurnal (day)
Antennae	Feathery	Clubbed
Body	Heavy Hairy	Sleek Smooth
Pupal structure	Cocoon	Chrysalis
Resting position	Wings spread	Wings folded

Butterfly

folded

Antennae   Body   Resting

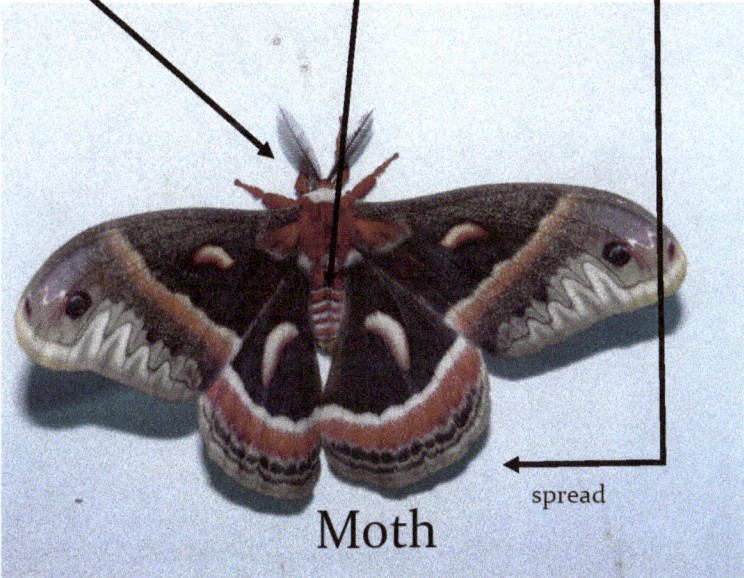

spread

Moth

Cocoon or Chrysalis

As shown previously, moths pupate in a cocoon while butterflies pupate as a chrysalis. The photo below shows an Atlas Moth sitting on the cocoon it had emerged from. Butterfly caterpillars change into a chrysalis. On the bottom of the next page is a photo of a Monarch butterfly chrysalis.

The cocoon is created by the moth caterpillar, spinning silk from the outside in, such that the caterpillar is ultimately trapped within the cocoon. At that point, the caterpillar changes into a pupa inside of the cocoon. If one cuts into a cocoon they will find the pupa from which the moth will eventually emerge. Shown at the top of the next page is the pupa of a Hubbard's Small Silkmoth.

Atlas Moth and cocoon

Moth pupa

Some moths, the Sphinx Moths for example, do not spin a cocoon, but rather the caterpillar digs a hole in the soil and pupates underground.

Butterfly chrysalis

Moth Anatomy
This photo shows the different structures that are commonly used in moth identification.

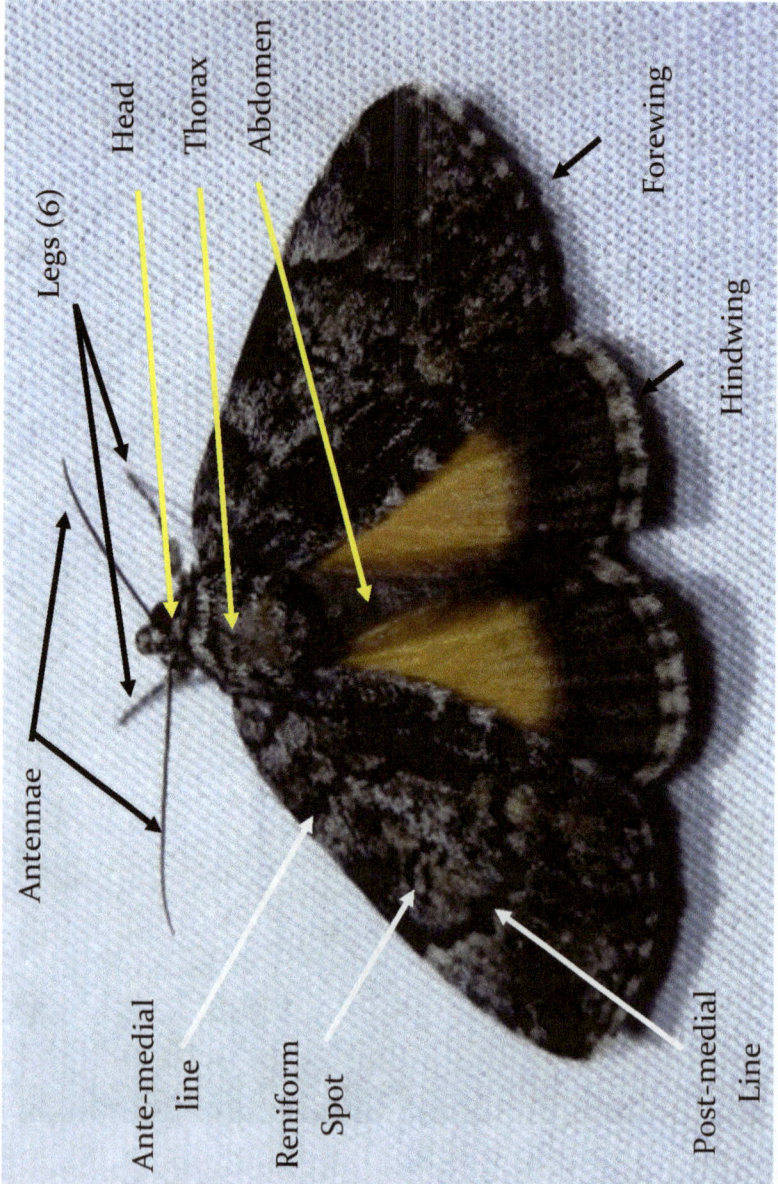

Another fun way to engage with moths is to search for their caterpillars. Many moth caterpillars fluoresce, in other words glow when exposed to ultraviolet light. Ultraviolet flashlights are available through many online retailers.

We have found one of the best times to go caterpillar hunting is in late summer and early autumn. The photos below were taken in early October. Examining the trees and brambles may yield some exciting surprises. But be sure to watch out for the stinging hairs and spines that several moth caterpillars use for defense.

Pictured below is the same caterpillar under ultraviolet light and the standard camera flash.

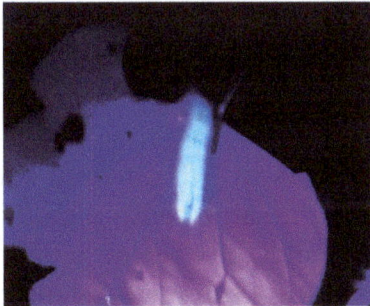

Attracting Moths

Since moths are largely nocturnal, special equipment is required to attract them for observation and study. While some people use the porch light as a tool to attract moths, I prefer something more portable.

At Butterfly Ridge we use a portable scaffolding made from one-inch pvc pipe (pictured on the next page). We hang the sheet from the crossbar of the scaffolding and attach it to the scaffolding with black, foam pipe insulation.

The scaffolding has two arms that extend from the top crossbar. The arms are angled to hold a light in front of each side of the sheet. From one arm we hang an ultraviolet tube light. From the other arm we hang a 250-watt mercury vapor light. These lights can be purchased from biological supply houses.

We power the lights in two different ways. We can either plug them into an extension cord run from the house or an outbuilding. We can plug in both lights simultaneously using a three-way adapter.

We also have a 2000 watt Honda generator that we can plug the lights into. The generator weighs only 30 pounds making it relatively portable and it can operate for about seven hours on a single tank of gas. By making the "rig" portable, we are able to survey moths in a variety of habitats and locations.

Moths, and also butterflies to a degree, can be attracted by painting a bait on tree trunks and stumps. The most common form of bait is a mixture of one-third beer, one-third maple syrup, and one-third ground fruit.

Moths as Pollinators

Frequently moths are not thought of as pollinators. Granted, while they may not be the pollinating machines that bees are, moths do provide pollinating services.

Perhaps the most famous moth pollinator is *Xanthopan morgana,* also known as Morgan's Sphinx Moth. Morgan's Sphinx is the pollinator of the Darwin Orchid. This beautiful orchid has an extremely long spur and Darwin predicted that the pollinator of the orchid was a moth with nearly a foot -long proboscis.

Darwin was much ridiculed for putting forth the idea that a moth could have such a long proboscis. However, over 40 years after Darwin's prediction, Morgan's Sphinx Moth was observed pollinating the Darwin Orchid.

While southeast Ohio does not have such tall tales of pollinating moths with enormous proboscises, our moths perform the service of pollination all the same. The most common example of this is normally found during the daytime hours as the clearwing moths visit long tubular flowers as shown by the photos of the Hummingbird and Snowberry Clearwing Moths on the next page.

For an example of nocturnal moths performing pollination, visit a blooming patch of Common

Hummingbird Clearwing Moth

SnowberryClearwing Moth

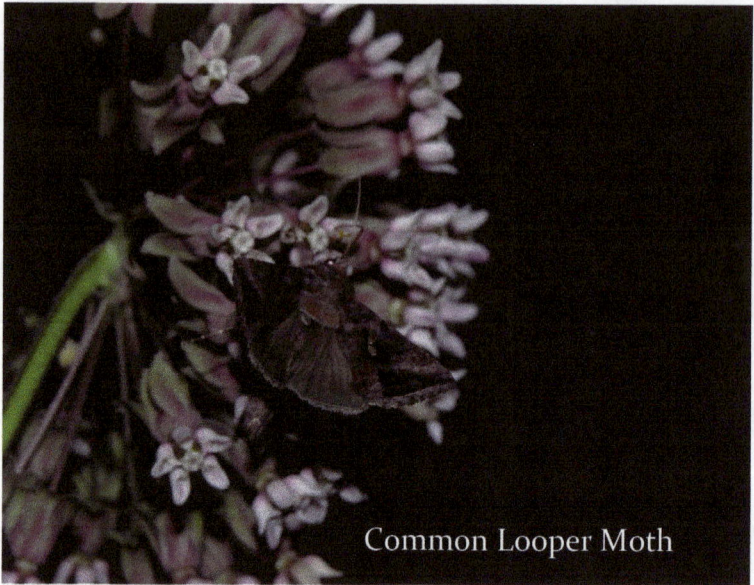

Common Looper Moth

Milkweed some evening. Above is a photo of a Common Looper Moth visiting Common Milkweed around 10pm on a June evening. This particular milkweed patch was being visited by several species of Owlet Moths as well as a Grass-veneer Moth.

What are Micromoths?

Micromoth is the term that is applied to moth species with Hodges Numbers between 0000 and 6234. Most of the moths in this group are quite small, sometimes no longer than a quarter-inch. However, some members of the Micromoths, for example the Carpenterworm Moths, can be well over an inch long.

Moth Myths

Moths have a significant public relations problem. There are many myths out there that put moths in a negative light. Let's refute many of those myths:

1. **All Moths Eat Clothes.** Of the thousands of moth species native to North America, there are only three who tend to damage clothing; the Common Clothes Moth, Case-bearing Clothes Moth, and Carpet Moth.
2. **Moths Bite.** In fact, many species of moths do not have functioning mouth parts. They do not feed on anything. Those who do have mouths have a proboscis which is designed to sip nectar from flowers.
3. **Moths are Harbingers of Death.** This myth is drawn from Central American folklore which claims that the presence of a Black Witch moth in the house means someone will die. The Black Witch is no different than any other moth and cannot predict death.
4. **Moths Spit.** Once again, moth mouths are designed to suck nectar, not spit.
5. **Female Moths Shoot Eggs at People.** While it is true that female moths are not always picky about what they lay eggs upon, they do not launch eggs as a defense mechanism.
6. **All Moths are Pests.** While there are some moth species that are agricultural and forest pests like Gypsy Moth and Corn Earworm Moth, an over-whelming majority of moth species live as a part

Black Witch

of nature, providing pollinating services and food for other organisms.

7. **Moths are Little, Brown, and Ugly.** Check out the Giant Silkworm Moth section of this book to refute this myth. Or simply look at the cover of this book!

Quick Reference to Families

Burrowing Webworm Moths
Page 22

Ribbed Cocoon-maker Moths
Page 24

Leaf Blotch Miner Moths
Page 24

Twirler Moths
Page 26

Ermine Moths
Page 36

Bristle-legged Moths
Page 38

Clearwing Moths
Page 40

Carpenter Moths
Page 42

Leafroller Moths
Page 42

Smoky Moths
Page 66

Flannel Moths
Page 68

Slug Caterpillar Moths
Page 70

Planthopper Parasite Moths
Page 78

Grass Moths
Page 80

Snout Moths
Page 100

Picture-wing Leaf Moths
Page 112

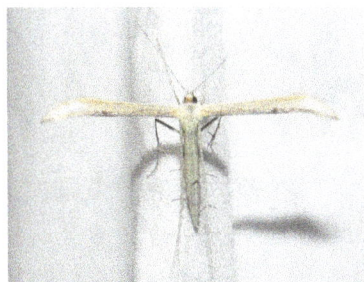

Plume Moths
Page 112

Hooktip Moths
Page 118

Inch-worm Moths
Page 120

Sack-bearer Moths
Page 168

Silkworm Moths
Page 170

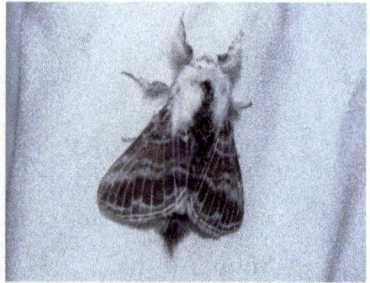

Tent Caterpillar Moths
Page 172

Giant Silkworm Moths
Page 174

Sphinx Moths
Page 186

Prominent Moths
Page 202

Tiger Moths
Page 214

Tussock Moths
Page 228

Owlet Moths
Page 230

Acrolophidae - Burrowing Webworm Moths
The larva of this family of moths makes tube-shaped nests in the soil near the roots they feed upon.

0340 – *Acrolophus arcanella*
Eastern Grass Tubeworm Moth

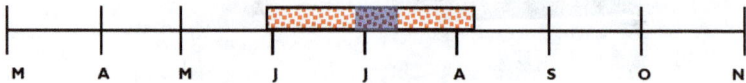

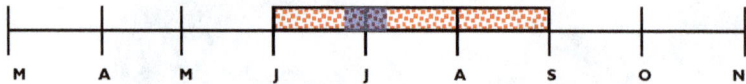

| M | A | M | J | J | A | S | O | N |

Host: Roots of clovers
Identification: Random small white spots on the forewings and shorter palps (mohawk!) separate this species from the other two *Acrolophus*.

0372 – *Acrolophus plumifrontella*
Eastern Grass Tubeworm Moth

| M | A | M | J | J | A | S | O | N |

Host: Roots of various grasses
Identification: Note the two dark squares on the brown background and the "mohawk" hairstyle. Caterpillar constructs silky webs near the roots of grasses. Does not cause significant damage to grasses.

0373 - *Acrolophus popeanella*
Clemens' Grass Tubeworm Moth

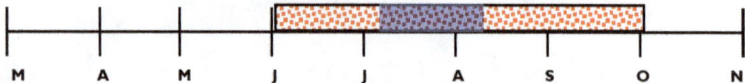

| M | A | M | J | J | A | S | O | N |

Host: Red clover
Identification: This species can be quite variable but the distinguishing features when compared to the Eastern Grass Tubeworm are the more prominent pair of spots on the forewing and checkering on the margins of the wing.

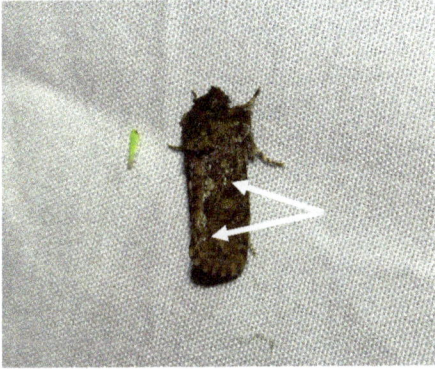

0340 – *Acrolophus arcanella*
Grass Tubeworm Moth

0372 – *Acrolophus plumifrontella*
Eastern Grass Tubeworm Moth

0373 – *Acrolophus popeanella*
Clemens' Grass Tubeworm Moth

Bucculatricidae - Ribbed Cocoon-maker Moths

This family gets its name from the longitudinal ridges on the cocoon. All start out as leaf miners.

0577 – *Bucculatrix pomifoliella*
Apple Skeletonizer Moth

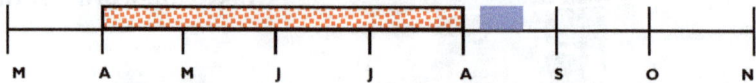

| M | A | M | J | J | A | S | O | N |

Host: Apple (leaves).

Identification: Larva starts out as a leaf miner, then feeds on upper leaf surface in later instars. Overwinters as cocoon. The dark brown spot at the edge of the forewing is consistent throughout this genus.

Gracillariidae - Leafblotch Miner Moths

This family is known for having especially long antennae and standing with the front of the body elevated.

0630 – *Caloptilia rhoifoliella*
Sumac Leafblotch MinerMoth

| M | A | M | J | J | A | S | O | N |

Host: Sumac.

Identification: Larva starts out as a leaf miner, but then in later instars becomes a leaf roller, rolling the leaf tip into a cone. The long, narrow gray appearance is unique among these small moths. The adult is roughly one centimeter in length.

0577 – Bucculatrix pomifoliella
Apple Skeletonizer Moth

Leafblotch Miner Moths

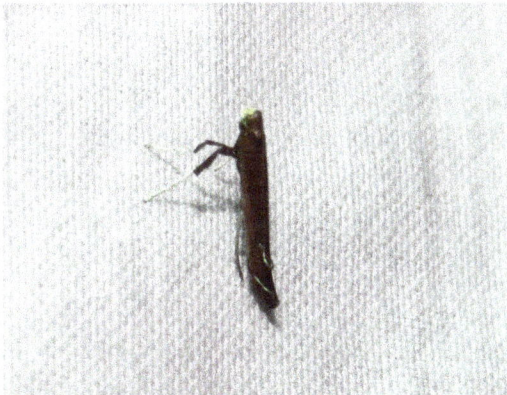

0630 – Caloptilia rhoifoliella
Sumac Leafblotch MinerMoth

Gelechioidae - Twirler Moths

The Twirler Moths have long, curved mouth parts in common. Typically they have small, fringed hindwings, but the hindwings are normally concealed by the forewings.

....

0874.1 – *Agonopterix alstroemeriana*
Poison Hemlock Moth

M	A	M	J	J	A	S	O	N

Host: Poison hemlock

Identification: The cream-colored patch on the head and extending down the "shoulders" is very distinctive. This moth is native to Europe and was introduced to North America in the 1970's.

....

0882 – *Agonopterix robiniella*
Four-dotted Agonopterix Moth

M	A	M	J	J	A	S	O	N

Host: Black locust

Identification: This moth is easily recognized by the gold and brown mottling of the wings with a conspicuous dark dot on each forewing. There can also be a dark diamond-shaped marking in the middle when the wings are closed.

0874.1 – Agonopterix alstroemeriana
Poison Hemlock Moth

0882 – Agonopterix robiniella
Four-dotted Agonopterix Moth

0912 – Semioscopis packardella
Packard's Concealer Moth

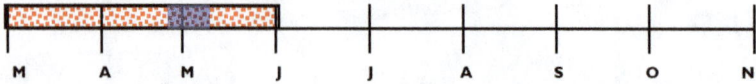

| M | A | M | J | J | A | S | O | N |

Host: Hawthorn and cherry
Identification: The two dark wavy lines running down the hindwing are quite unique and hard to miss. This moth is rarely found in southeast Ohio despite an abundance of host plants.

1011 – Antaerotricha schlaegeri
Schlaeger's Fruitworm Moth

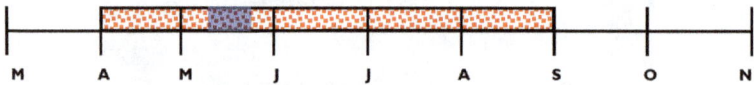

| M | A | M | J | J | A | S | O | N |

Host: White oak
Identification: This is a surprisingly large moth with a wing span of nearly an inch. Schlaeger's is referred to as a bird-dropping moth because of its appearance. It is the largest of the bird-dropping moths that we have found at Butterfly Ridge.

1046 – Epicallima argenticinctella
Orange-headed Epicallima Moth

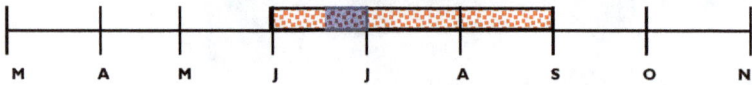

| M | A | M | J | J | A | S | O | N |

Host: Unknown
Identification: Very little is known about this moth. With a wingspan of about a centimeter, this is one of the most colorful of the micromoths at Butterfly Ridge.

0912 – *Semioscopis
packardella*
Packard's Concealer Moth

1011 – *Antaeotricha
schlaegeri*
**Schlaeger's Fruitworm
Moth**

1046 – *Epicallima
argenticinctella*
**Orange-headed
Epicallima Moth**

1261 – Coleophora querciella

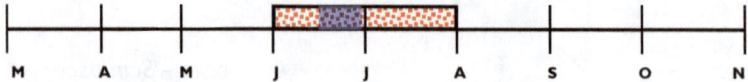

M A M J J A S O N

Host: Oak, cherry, basswood
Identification: Very little is known about this moth.

....

1387 – Coleophora mayrella
Metallic Coleophora Moth

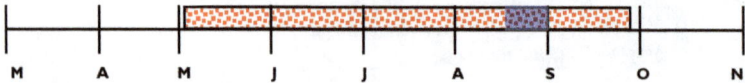

M A M J J A S O N

Host: Clover
Identification: Note that the base of each antennae is thickened. Beyond the thickening the antennae are ringed in brown and white. As the name implies, this moth has metallic wings.

....

1479 – Cosmopterix dapifera

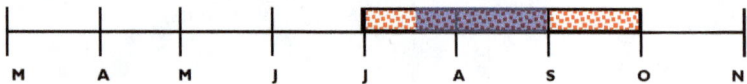

M A M J J A S O N

Host: Unknown
Identification: Very little is known about this moth, but it is certainly a colorful addition to Butterfly Ridge. There are several members of *Cosmopterix* that are very similar in appearance.

....

1722 – Theisoa constrictella

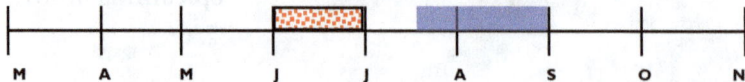

M A M J J A S O N

Host: Elm
Identification: The brown horizontal line across the forewings, combined with two brown patches near the tip of each forewing are very distinctive on this very tiny moth.

1261 – Coleophora querciella

1387 – Coleophora mayrella
Metallic Coleophora Moth

1479 – Cosmopterix dapifera

1722 – Theisoa constrictella

1834 – Sinoe robiniella

M	A	M	J	J	A	S	O	N

Host: Black locust, honeylocust, and indigo bush.

Identification: The dark 'boomerang' when the wings are closed is distinctive. Otherwise, very little is known about this moth.

1840 – Exoteleia pinifoliella
Pine Needleminer Moth

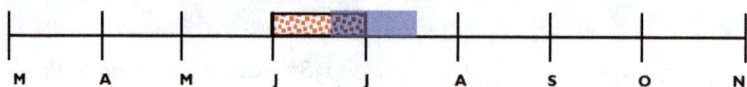

M	A	M	J	J	A	S	O	N

Host: Pine

Identification: Note the multiple horizontal brown bars. This species overwinters as a larva inside the pine needle.

1862 – Pseudochelaria pennsylvanica

M	A	M	J	J	A	S	O	N

Host: Unknown

Identification: Very little is known about this moth. Identification is straight forward with a dark shield the extends at the edges.

1864 – Pseudochelaria walsinghami

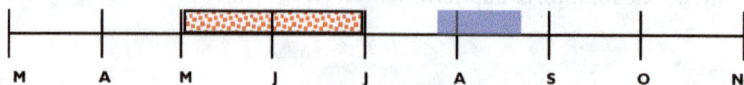

M	A	M	J	J	A	S	O	N

Host: Staghorn sumac

Identification: This moth looks much like the previous species except that there is a definite break between the shield and the vertical streaks. Otherwise, little is known about this species.

1834 – Sinoe robiniella

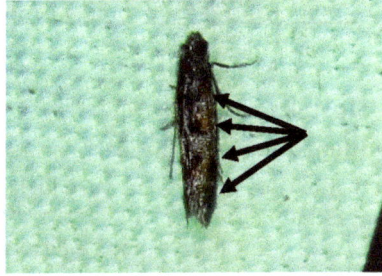

1840 – Exoteleia pinifoliella
Pine Needleminer Moth

1862 – Pseudochelaria pennsylvanica

1864 – Pseudochelaria walsinghami

2093 – Chionodes mediofuscella
Black-smudged Chionodes Moth

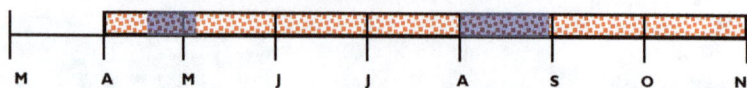

| | | | | | | | | | |
|M|A|M|J|J|A|S|O|N|

Host: Ragweed
Identification: The dark smudging on the forewing margin is distinctive. Otherwise, very little is known about this moth.

2204 – Fascista cercerisella
Redbud Leaffolder Moth

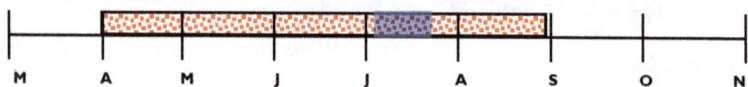

| | | | | | | | | | |
|M|A|M|J|J|A|S|O|N|

Host: Redbud
Identification: Note the white head and four white spots on each forewing. This species overwinters as a pupa in the leaf litter.

2229 – Battaristis vittella
Stripe-backed Moth

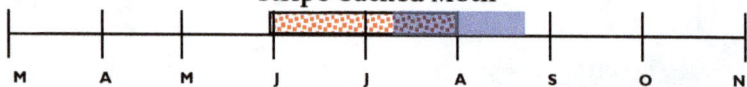

| | | | | | | | | | |
|M|A|M|J|J|A|S|O|N|

Host: Pine
Identification: Very similar to the Pine Needleminer (1840) but there is much greater color contrast in the stripes of this species.

2295 – Dichomeris flavocostella
Cream-edged Dichomeris Moth

| | | | | | | | | | |
|M|A|M|J|J|A|S|O|N|

Host: Aster and goldenrod
Identification: The cream-colored stripe on the black background is very unique among our Ohio moths.

2093 – Chionodes mediofuscella
Black-smudged Chionodes Moth

2204 – Fascista cercerisella
Redbud Leaffolder Moth

2229 – Battaristis vittella
Stripe-backed Moth

2295 – Dichomeris flavocostella
Cream-edged Dichomeris Moth

2307 – Dichomeris nonstrigella
The Little Devil

| M | A | M | J | J | A | S | O | N |

Host: Aster

Identification: This moth is quite small, only 7-8 millimeters in length. It is completely black except for orange palps.

Yponometoidae - Ermine Moths

This is a family of small to medium size moths. The larva tend to nest and feed in communal webs.

2353 – Homadaula anisocentra
Mimosa Webworm Moth

| M | A | M | J | J | A | S | O | N |

Host: Mimosa and honeylocust

Identification: A very small moth that is steel color with random black spots. Native to Japan and China. First found in the US in 1943.

2401 – Atteva aurea
Ailanthus Webworm Moth

| M | A | M | J | J | A | S | O | N |

Host: Tree of heaven and sumac

Identification: The orange stripes on the back and white checkerboard background in unlike any moth in our area. Possibly the most common moth at Butterfly Ridge, at times coming to the sheet by the hundreds.

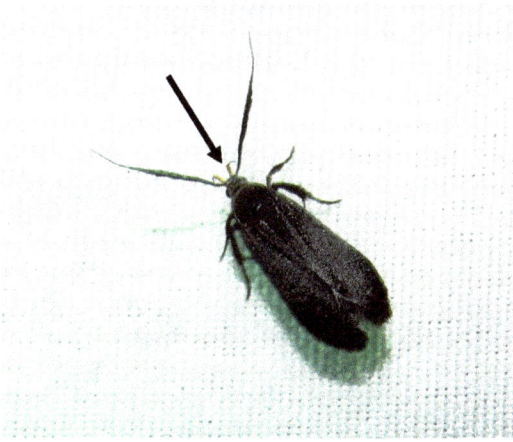

2307 – *Dichomeris nonstrigella*
The Little Devil

2353 – *Homadaula anisocentra*
Mimosa Webworm Moth

2401 - *Atteva aurea*
Ailanthus Webworm Moth

2413 - *Swammerdamia caesiella*

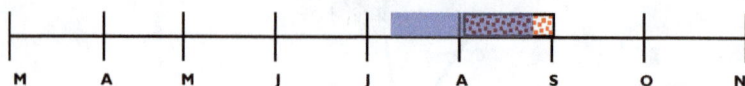

Host: Birch

Identification: This species looks similar to Mimosa Webworm, however this species has a distinctive white head.

....

2467 - *Argyresthia oreasella*
Cherry Shoot Borer Moth

Host: Cherry

Identification: The contrasting brown/gold color on the clean white background is distinctive for this species, as is the headstand position!

Schreckensteinioidea - Bristle-legged Moths

This family of moths is represented at Butterfly Ridge by a single species of *Schreckensteinia*. The family is named for the stout spines on the hindlegs.

....

2507 - *Schreckensteinia erythriella*

Host: Sumac

Identification: This tiny, unmarked, gray moth is recognized by the stout spines on its legs. One of our smallest moths with a body length of barely six millimeters.

2413 - *Swammerdamia caesiella*

2467 - *Argyresthia oreasella*
Cherry Shoot Borer Moth

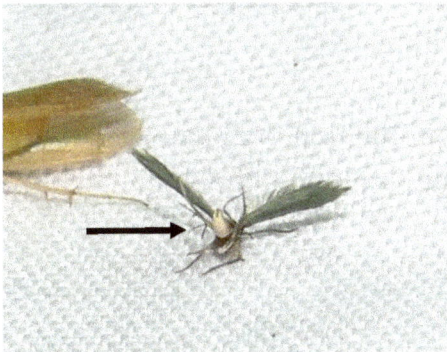

2507 - *Schreckensteinia erythriella*

Sesiidae - Clearwing Moths

This family of moths is represented at Butterfly Ridge by a single species of *Synanthedon*.

··

2554 - Synanthedon acerni
Maple Callus Borer Moth

M	A	M	J	J	A	S	O	N

Host: Maple

Identification: This is a wasp mimic. Look for the black wing stripes and tuft of orange hairs at the tip of the abdomen. This moth is regularly seen, albeit in low numbers, in late spring and early summer. The caterpillars bore into maple trees to feed, as the tree forms a callus around them.

··

2596 – Carmenta bassiformis
Ironweed Clearwing Moth

M	A	M	J	J	A	S	O	N

Host: Ironweed

Identification: This moth is a wasp-mimic. Keep in mind that bees and wasps normally have shorter antennae than this and wasps normally have a section of abdomen that is very thin.

2554 - *Synanthedon acerni*
Maple Callus Borer Moth

2596 - *Carmenta bassiformis*
Ironweed Clearwing Moth

Cossidae - Carpenterworm Moths

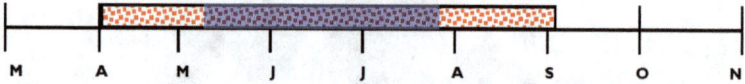

Most of the members of this family are found in Asia. Members of the Cossidae have larva that are wood borers. Large moths that are included in the micromoth group.

2693 - *Prionoxystus robiniae*
Carpenterworm Moth

| M | A | M | J | J | A | S | O | N |

Host: Black locust
Identification: Initially this large moth may look like a member of the sphinx moths. The strongly reticulate (veiny) pattern of the wings is unlike any of the sphinxs. The checkered wing margin is also very different from the sphinx moths.

Tortricidae - Leafroller Moths

As the family name implies, the caterpillars of these moths roll the leaf and nest inside. These moths are frequently no more than a centimeter long.

2711 - *Paralobesia liriodendrana*
Tuliptree Leaftier Moth

| M | A | M | J | J | A | S | O | N |

Host: Tuliptree and magnolia
Identification: The lilac color on the front half of this moth is very distinctive. This species is a leaf skeletonizer.

2693 - *Prionoxystus robiniae*
Carpenterworm Moth

Leafroller Moths

2711 - *Paralobesia liriodendrana*
Tuliptree Leaftier Moth

2749 - *Eumarozia malachitana*
Sculptured Moth

Host: Persimmon and pear
Identification: This moth has a very unique color scheme with olive over the front half, pink over the back half.

2771 - *Phaecasiophora confixana*
Macrame Moth

Host: Unknown
Identification: Small with wingspan much less than an inch. Dark brown spots on light brown background.

2772 - *Phaecasiophora niveiguttana*
Labyrinth Moth

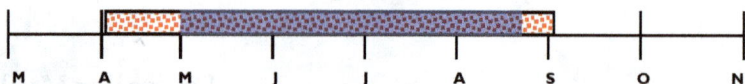

Host: Sassafras and witchhazel
Identification: Small with wingspan much less than an inch. Dark brown spots on light brown background. Very little is known about this moth.

2898 - *Retinia gemistrigulana*

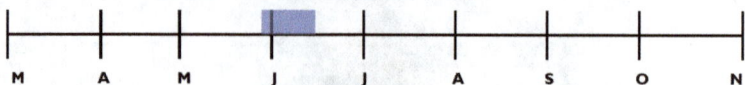

Host: Pine
Identification: This moth is steel color with dark horizontal striping. Little is known of this species.

2749 - *Eumarozia malachitana*
Sculptured Moth

2771 - *Phaecasiophora confixana*
Macramé Moth

2772 – *Phaecasiophora niveiguttana*

Labyrinth Moth

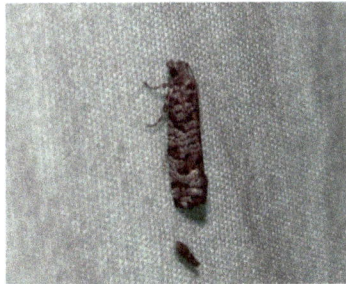

2898 - *Retinia gemistrigulana*

2928 - *Eucosma raracana*
Reddish Phaneta Moth

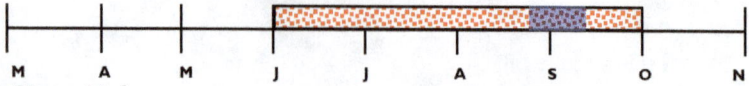

| M | A | M | J | J | A | S | O | N |

Host: Unknown

Identification: This small moth is easily recognized by magenta wings with buff-colored tips. Little is known about this moth.

2929 - *Eucosma ochroterminana*
Buff-tipped Moth

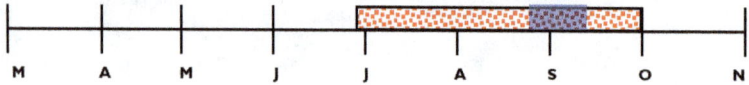

| M | A | M | J | J | A | S | O | N |

Host: Unknown

Identification: Much like the previous species with buff-colored wing tips, however the rest of the wing is a dark brown almost black. Little is known about this moth.

2937 - *Eucosma parmatana*
Aster Eucosma Moth

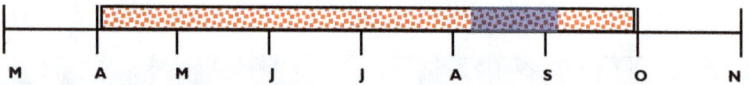

| M | A | M | J | J | A | S | O | N |

Host: Aster

Identification: On this moth, look for the two conspicuous white spots (with wings closed) on an otherwise dark background.

3074 - *Eucopina tocullionana*
White Pinecone Borer Moth

| M | A | M | J | J | A | S | O | N |

Host: Pine

Identification: The forewings of this moth feature alternating red and yellow bands with a checked wind edge.

2928 - *Eucosma raracana*
Reddish Phaneta Moth

2929 - *Eucosma ochroterminana*
Buff-tipped Moth

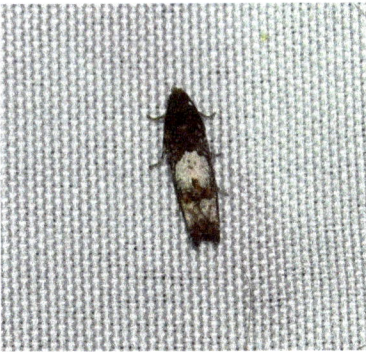

2937 - *Eucosma parmatana*
Aster Eucosma Moth

3074 - *Eucopina tocullionana*
White Pinecone Borer Moth

3233 - *Proteoteras crescentata*
Northern Boxelder Twig Borer Moth

M A M J J A S O N

Host: Boxelder

Identification: Look for the dark 'swoosh' on the margin of the forewing. This moth is common where boxelder plantings are found.

3273 - *Chimoptesis pennsylvaniana*
Filigreed Moth

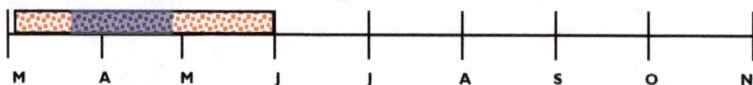

M A M J J A S O N

Host: Unknown

Identification: Small with diamonds across the top. Very little is known about this moth.

3366 - *Ancylis laciniana*

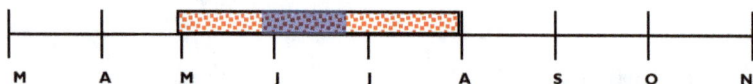

M A M J J A S O N

Host: Unknown

Identification: This small moth is easily recognized by the rust-colored spot on top.

3375 - *Ancylis divisana*
Two-toned Ancylis Moth

M A M J J A S O N

Host: Oak and sycamore

Identification: Rusty-brown color on the front half and straw-colored on the back half with a very thin silver line separating the two.

3233 - *Proteoteras crescentata*
Northern Boxelder Twig Borer

3273 – *Chimoptesis pennsylvaniana*
Filigreed Moth

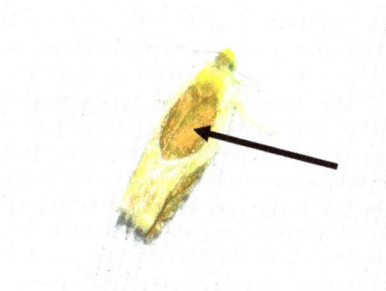

3366 - *Ancylis laciniana*

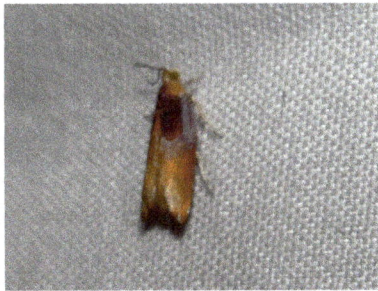

3375 - *Ancylis divisana*
Two-toned Ancylis Moth

3377 - *Ancylis muricana*
Red-headed Ancylis Moth

M	A	M	J	J	A	S	O	N

Host: Unknown

Identification: The front half is very dark. Look for the contrasting red head. Very little is known about this moth.

3406 - *Dichrorampha bittana*

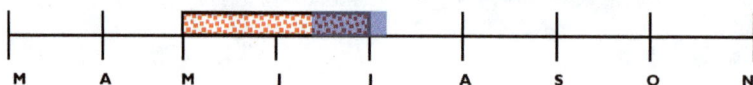

M	A	M	J	J	A	S	O	N

Host: Aster

Identification: This moth is very distinctive. Front half is dark, back half is gold/orange. Also look for silver striping near forewing tip and dark marginal spots.

3446 - *Corticivora clarki*

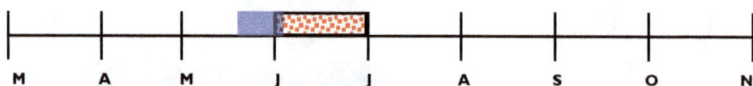

M	A	M	J	J	A	S	O	N

Host: Pine

Identification: This small moth is easily recognized by the gray base color with alternating thick and thin dark bands.

3486 - *Cydia toreuta*
Eastern Pine Seedworm Moth

M	A	M	J	J	A	S	O	N

Host: Pine

Identification: This moth has a gray base color with metallic horizontal bands. Only a few records from Ohio.

3377 - *Ancylis muricana*
Red-headed Ancylis Moth

3406 - *Dichrorampha bittana*

3446 - *Corticivora clarki*

3486 - *Cydia toreuta*
**Eastern Pine Seedworm
Moth**

3494 - *Clydia latiferreana*
Filbertworm Moth

M	A	M	J	J	A	S	O	N

Host: Fruit of oak, beech, and possibly filbert.

Identification: Small. This moth is easily recognized by the silver-metallic stripes on the rust-colored base. While it is questioned whether Filbertworm uses Filbert as a host, at Butterfly Ridge this moth is largely found near Filbert trees.

3495 - *Gymandrosoma punctidiscanum*
Dotted Ecdytolopha Moth

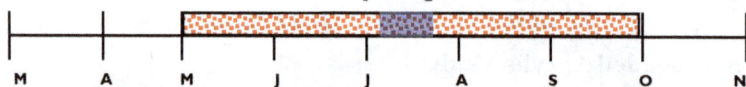

M	A	M	J	J	A	S	O	N

Host: Black locust and oak

Identification: This moth has white frosting toward the tip of the forewing and a distinct white spot in the middle of the wing.

3497 - *Ecdytolopha insiticiana*
Locust Twig Borer Moth

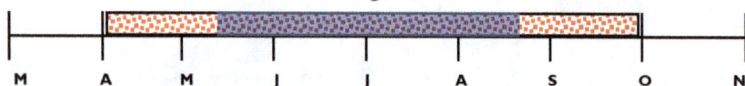

M	A	M	J	J	A	S	O	N

Host: Black locust and wisteria

Identification: Small with wingspan much less than an inch. Bicolored wings, dark toward the head, white toward the wing tips. Bright red caterpillar feeds within the twigs.

3540 - *Acleris placidana*

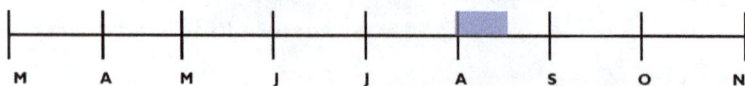

M	A	M	J	J	A	S	O	N

Host: Birch

Identification: A very bland pale moth with dark spots on the forewings, occasionally these spots join to form a triangle.

3494 – *Cydia latiferreana*
Filbertworm Moth

3495 - *Gymandrosoma punctidiscanum*
Dotted Ecdytolopha Moth

3497 – *Ecdytolopha insiticiana*
Locust Twig Borer Moth

3540 - *Acleris placidana*

3542 - *Acleris flavivittana*
Multiform Leafroller Moth

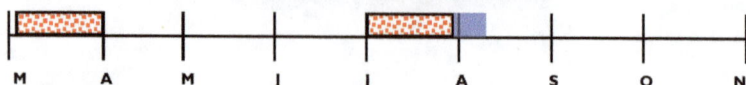

| M | A | M | J | J | A | S | O | N |

Host: Apple and cherry

Identification: This moth comes in a wide variety of color schemes but what they all seem to have in common is a pale stripe along the upper margin of the forewing.

....

3593 - *Pandemis lamprosana*
Woodgrain Leafroller Moth

| M | A | M | J | J | A | S | O | N |

Host: Several deciduous trees

Identification: Very similar to the Three-lined Moth. The Woodgrain Leafroller has dark speckling in the wings plus the small spot near the tip of the forewing is less complete than it is in the Three-lined.

....

3594 - *Pandemis limitata*
Three-lined Leafroller Moth

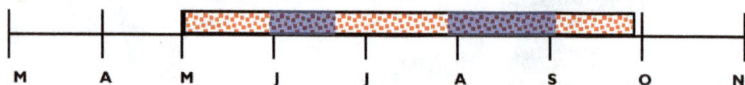

| M | A | M | J | J | A | S | O | N |

Host: Several deciduous trees

Identification: Very similar to the Woodgrained Leafroller. The Three-lined Leafroller lacks dark speckling in the wings plus the small spot near the tip of the forewing is more complete than it is in the Woodgrain.

Leafroller Moths

3542 - *Acleris flavivittana*
Multiform Leafroller Moth

3593 - *Pandemis lamprosana*
Woodgrain Leafroller Moth

3594 - *Pandemis limitata*
Three-lined Leafroller Moth

3597 - *Argyrotaenia velutinana*
Red-banded Leafroller Moth

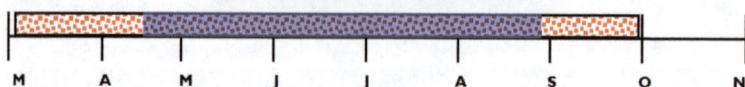

| | | | | | | | | |
|M|A|M|J|J|A|S|O|N|

Host: Fruit trees (leaves and fruit)
Identification: Small. Red-brown band diagonal across wings.
Overwinters as a pupa. Considered a pest in fruit orchards.

3603 - *Argyrotaenia tabulana*
Jack Pine Tube Moth

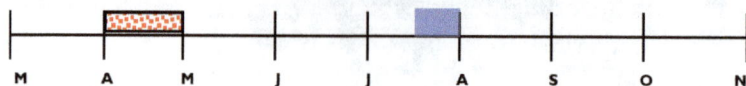

| | | | | | | | | |
|M|A|M|J|J|A|S|O|N|

Host: Pine
Identification: This moth is very similar to White Pinecone
Borer Moth (3074). Look for the teardrop-shaped cut-outs in the
red bands.

3624 - *Argyrotaenia alisellana*
White-spotted Leafroller Moth

| | | | | | | | | |
|M|A|M|J|J|A|S|O|N|

Host: Oak
Identification: This moth has a very bold pattern not soon for-
gotten or confused with anything else; a brown paintball 'splat'
on a white background!

3625 - *Argyrotaenia mariana*
Gray-banded Leafroller Moth

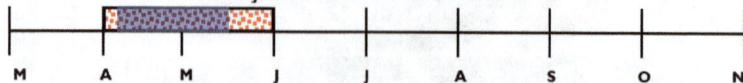

| | | | | | | | | |
|M|A|M|J|J|A|S|O|N|

Host: Several species of deciduous trees
Identification: The characteristic feature of this moth is the
dark triangular markings at the leading edge of the forewings.
Similar to *Acleris placidana* (3540).

3597 – *Argyrotaenia velutinana*
Red-banded Leafroller Moth

3603 - *Argyrotaenia tabulana*
Jack Pine Tube Moth

3624 - *Argyrotaenia alisellana*
White-spotted Leafroller

3625 – *Argyrotaenia mariana*
**Gray-banded
Leafroller Moth**

3632 - *Choristoneura fractivittana*
Broken-banded Leafroller Moth

M A M J J A S O N

Host: Several deciduous trees

Identification: True to its name, the dark bands on the forewing are broken. In Ohio, we have a single generation of this moth.

3633 - *Choristoneura parallela*
Parallel-banded Leafroller Moth

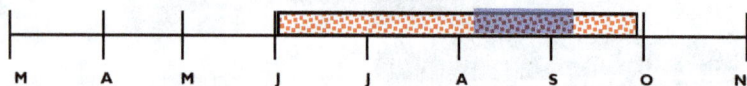

M A M J J A S O N

Host: A wide variety of plants from deciduous trees to forbs.
Identification: The obvious parallel bands make this moth easy to identify.

3635 - *Choristoneura rosaceana*
Oblique-banded Leafroller Moth

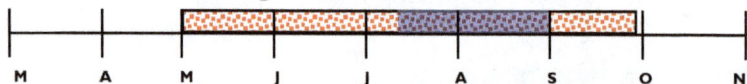

M A M J J A S O N

Host: The Rose Family including apples, pears, and peaches
Identification: The banding on this moth, while similar to the previous, is not as precisely paralleled. Also, the dark spot on the back of the thorax is fairly consistent.

3643 - *Choristoneura pinus*
Jack Pine Budworm Moth

M A M J J A S O N

Host: Pine

Identification: This moth differs from the other red Tortricids by lacking distinct bands. Frequently there is a small white patch on the leading edge of the forewing (absent in this photo).

3632 - *Choristoneura fractivittana*
Broken-banded Leafroller Moth

3633 - *Choristoneura parallela*
Parallel-banded Leafroller Moth

3635 - *Choristoneura rosaceana*
Oblique-banded Leafroller Moth

3643 - *Choristoneura pinus*
Jack Pine Budworm Moth

3672 - *Syndemis afflictana*
Gray Leafroller Moth

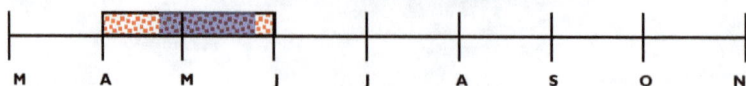

| M | | A | | M | | J | | J | | A | | S | | O | | N |

Host: Fir, birch, maple, and apple

Identification: Small. Overall appearance is dark gray with a light gray or silvery band that runs perpendicular across the wings.

3688 - *Clepsis peritana*
Garden Tortrix Moth

| M | | A | | M | | J | | J | | A | | S | | O | | N |

Host: Strawberries and other low plants

Identification: Small. Overall appearance is dark gray with a light gray or silvery band that runs perpendicular across the wings.

3699 - *Sparganothis tristriata*
Three-streaked Sparganothis Moth

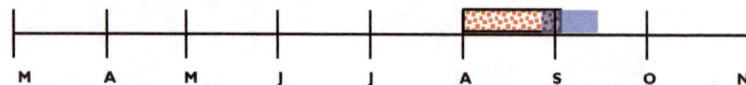

| M | | A | | M | | J | | J | | A | | S | | O | | N |

Host: Several species of evergreen trees

Identification: The rust colored stripes on the pale background is very unique for Ohio moths.

3720 - *Cenopis reticulatana*
Reticulated Fruitworm Moth

| M | | A | | M | | J | | J | | A | | S | | O | | N |

Host: Several species of deciduous trees

Identification: Small. The reticulate, or veiny, appearance of the wings is very unique. This moth also has more thick dark veins than any of the look-alikes.

3672 – Syndemis afflictana
Gray Leafroller Moth

3688 - Clepsis peritana
Garden Tortrix Moth

3699 - Sparganothis tristriata
Three-streaked Sparganothis Moth

3720 - Cenopis reticulatana
Reticulated Fruitworm Moth

3732 - *Platynota flavedana*
Black-shaded Platynota Moth

| M | A | M | J | J | A | S | O | N |

Host: A variety of woody and herbaceous plants
Identification: Small. This moth is sexually dimorphic. The male has what resembles an oily spot neat the top of the forewings. Females lack this and simply have dark banding.

3740 - *Platynota idaeusalis*
Tufted Apple Budmoth

| M | A | M | J | J | A | S | O | N |

Host: A wide variety of woody and herbaceous plants including apple
Identification: This moth has a gray base color with a reddish shield in the middle. This is one of the larger members of the Tortricids, with a wingspan around two centimeters.

3743 - *Platynota exasperatana*
Exasperating Platynota Moth

| M | A | M | J | J | A | S | O | N |

Host: Unknown
Identification: This moth is quite variable, but usually displaying pale color directly behind the head and near the apex of the forewings. The wings also have a roughened appearance. The name 'exasperating' relates to the roughened appearance, not frustrations in attempting to identify it!

Male

3732- *Platynota flavedana*

Black-shaded Platynota Moth

Female

3732- *Platynota flavedana*

Black-shaded Platynota Moth

3740 - *Platynota idaeusalis*

Tufted Apple Budmoth

3743 - *Platynota exasperatana*

Exasperating Platynota Moth

3747 - *Coelostathma discopunctana*
Batman Moth

Host: Unknown

Identification: Small. Looking at this moth upside-down might make visualizing the "Batman" common name a little easier. For having such a colorful name, there is little that is known about this moth.

3748 - *Amorbia humerosana*
White-line Leafroller Moth

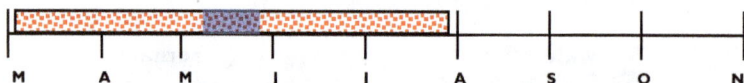

Host: A wide variety of plants including poison ivy!

Identification: This small moth is identified by the gray base color with black flecks throughout the forewing.

3754.2 - *Aethes argentilimitana*

Host: Unknown

Identification: A very striking tiny moth with silver-bordered gold bands across a white a background. Very little is known about the life cycle of this species.

3807 - *Phalonidia lepidana*

Host: Unknown

Identification: Another very striking moth with a clean brown band across a white background. Otherwise, little is known about this species.

3747 - *Coelostathma*
discopunctana
Batman Moth

3748 - *Amorbia humerosana*
White-line Leafroller Moth

3754.2 - *Aethes argentilimitana*

3807 - *Phalonidia lepidana*

3848 - *Atroposia oenotherana*
Primrose Cochylid Moth

```
M     A     M     J     J     A     S     O     N
```

Host: Primrose

Identification: This tiny beauty has a wingspan of barely one centimeter and the color combination is unlike any micromoth in our region. So little is known about this species that its scientific name is not yet official!

Zygaenidae - Smoky Moths

This family of moths is known for their smoky, dark, translucent wings.

4624 - *Harrisina americana*
Grapeleaf Skeletonizer Moth

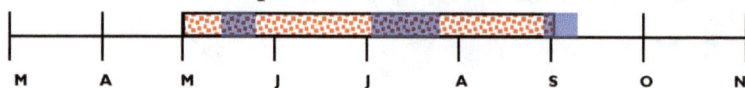

```
M     A     M     J     J     A     S     O     N
```

Host: Grape

Identification: Completely dark wasp-mimic except for colorful 'neck'. The caterpillar of this species skeletonizes grape leaves, eating all of the leaf tissue except for the leaf veins. Based on our observation data, we suspect this species has three generation per year.

4629 - *Acoloithus falsarius*
Clemens' False Skeletonizer Moth

```
M     A     M     J     J     A     S     O     N
```

Host: Grape

Identification: Completely dark wasp-mimic except for colorful 'neck'. Unlike previous species, the colorful neck has a black break on the back. The caterpillar of this species skeletonizes grape leaves, eating all of the leaf tissue except for the leaf veins.

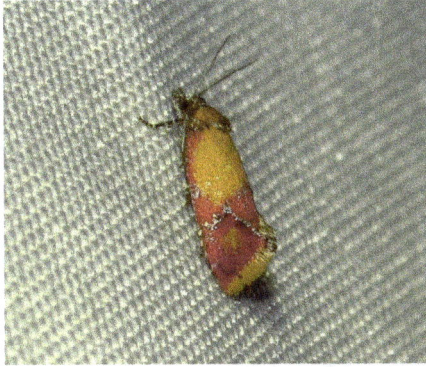

3848 - *Atroposia oenotherana*
Primrose Cochylid Moth

4624 – *Harrisina americana*
**Grapeleaf Skeletonizer
Moth**

4629 - *Acoloithus falsarius*
**Clemens' False Skeletonizer
Moth**

4639 - *Pyromorpha dimidiata*
Orange-patched Smoky Moth

M A M J J A S O N

Host: Leaf litter

Identification: This moth is thought to be a Lycid beetle mimic. The feathery antennae of the Smoky Moth distinguishes it from the beetle. Similar also to the Black and Yellow Lichen Moth which is found in our area. Wing color is noticeably different however.

Megalopygidae - Flannel Moths

As the common name implies, these moths are covered with dense, short hairs giving them a furry appearance.

4644 - *Lagoa crispata*
Black Waved Flannel Moth

M A M J J A S O N

Host: Several deciduous tree species

Identification: The black splotching on the side separates this species from other flannel moths. A common species at Butterfly Ridge during late spring and early summer. Flies early in the evening. Caterpillars have stinging spines.

4650 - *Norape ovina*
White Flannel Moth

M A M J J A S O N

Host: Black locust, hackberry, and redbud

Identification: This densely furry moth is pure white except for the golden antennae. Caterpillars have stinging spines.

4639 - *Pyromorpha dimidiata*
Orange-patched Smoky Moth

4644 - *Lagoa crispata*
Black Waved Flannel Moth

4650 - *Norape ovina*
White Flannel Moth

caterpillar

caterpillar

Limacodidae - Slug Caterpillar Moths

This family of moths is named for their slug-like caterpillars which can inflict a painful sting when disturbed. These moths are normally seen in early summer.

4654 - *Tortricidia flexuosa*
Abbreviated Button Slug Moth

```
M    A    M    J    J    A    S    O    N
```

Host: Maple, birch, cherry, oak

Identification: Note the varying dark splotching on otherwise solid yellow. Butterfly Ridge has also had sightings of Red-crossed Button Slug, which many experts debate whether it is a separate species from Abbreviated Button Slug.

4659 - *Packardia geminata*
Jeweled Tailed Slug Moth

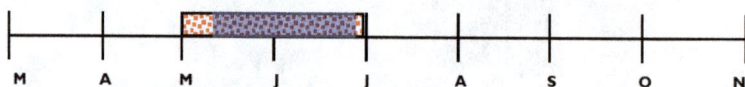

```
M    A    M    J    J    A    S    O    N
```

Host: Unknown

Identification: The bright white 'jewels' near the margin of the forewing set this slug moth apart from the others. Otherwise, little is known about this species.

4665 - *Lithacodes fasciola*
Yellow-shouldered Slug Moth

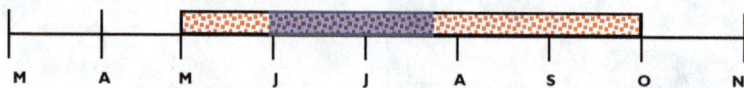

```
M    A    M    J    J    A    S    O    N
```

Host: Several deciduous tree species

Identification: The white, toothed line down the middle of the forewing is very distinctive among our slug moths.

4654 – *Tortricidia flexuosa*
**Abbreviated Button Slug
Moth**

4659 - *Packardia geminata*
Jeweled Tailed Slug Moth

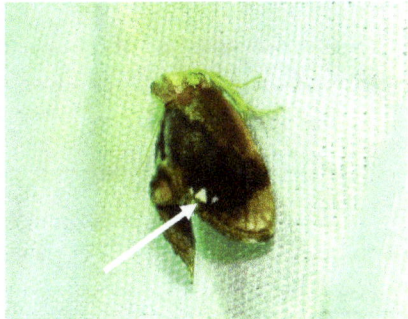

4665 - *Lithacodes fasciola*
**Yellow-shouldered
Slug Moth**

4667 - *Apoda y-inversum*
Yellow-collared Slug Moth

M A M J J A S O N

Host: Birch, ironwood, hickory, oak

Identification: Two parallel lines and one perpendicular line on the forewings resemble a 'v' shape. The yellow collar referenced in the common name applies to the slug-like caterpillar rather than the adult moth.

4669 - *Apoda biguttata*
Shagreened Slug Moth

M A M J J A S O N

Host: Ironwood, hickory, oak

Identification: The thick silver 'y' on each forewing is unique among our slug moths.

4671 - *Prolimacodes badia*
Skiff Moth

M A M J J A S O N

Host: A wide variety of deciduous trees and shrubs

Identification: The dark brown half-moon on the light brown background is distinctive. However, while not the same design, this moth shares the same basic color pattern as the Arcigera Flower Moth (Hodge #11128) which flies later in the season.

4667 - *Apoda y-inversum*
Yellow-collared Slug Moth

4669 - *Apoda biguttata*
Shagreened Slug Moth

4671 - *Prolimacodes badia*
Skiff Moth

4675 - *Isochaetes beutenmuelleri*
Spun Glass Slug Moth

| M | A | M | J | J | A | S | O | N |

Host: Swamp oak

Identification: Most references list swamp oak as the host plant, however Butterfly Ridge and vicinity does not have any swamp oak, so there must be another host. The 'brushy' appearance of the legs is distinctive. The common name is derived from the appearance of the caterpillar.

4677 - *Phobetron pithecium*
Hag or Monkey Slug Moth

| M | A | M | J | J | A | S | O | N |

Host: A wide variety of deciduous trees and shrubs

Identification: Very different in appearance to our other slug moths. The brightly-colored tuft of hairs on the middle pair of legs is quite distinctive on this bug. The caterpillar (from where the monkey slug name is derived) is quite an odd looking creature, sort of like a densely hairy, brown octopus!

4679 - *Natada nasoni*
Nason's Slug Moth

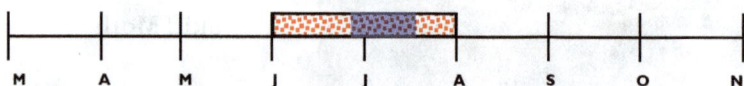

| M | A | M | J | J | A | S | O | N |

Host: Beech, hickory, hornbeam, oak

Identification: The two dark lines on the forewings run nearly parallel, almost meeting at the wing apex.

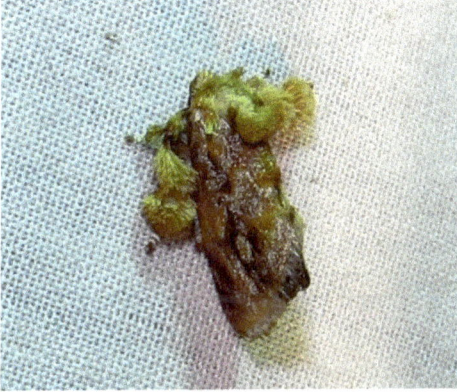

4675 - *Isochaetes beutenmuelleri*
Spun Glass Slug Moth

4677 - *Phobetron pithecium*
Hag or Monkey Slug Moth

4679 - *Natada nasoni*
Nason's Slug Moth

4681 - *Isa textula*
Crowned Slug Moth

| M | A | M | J | J | A | S | O | N |

Host: Primarily oak, but other trees as well.

Identification: Non-descript, but has the classic slug moth shape. The common name refers to the design of the stinging cells on the caterpillar.

4685 - *Adoneta spinuloides*
Purple-crested Slug Moth

| M | A | M | J | J | A | S | O | N |

Host: Several species of deciduous trees.

Identification: in a way similar to Yellow-shouldered Slug, but in this species the white line on the forewing is broken in the middle. Once again, the common name refers to attributes of the caterpillar.

4697 - *Euclea delphinii*
Spiny Oak-slug Moth

| M | A | M | J | J | A | S | O | N |

Host: A wide variety of deciduous trees and shrubs

Identification: Small green spots on the dark brown background is unique among Butterfly Ridge's moths.

4698 - *Parasa chloris*
Smaller Parasa Moth

| M | A | M | J | J | A | S | O | N |

Host: Apple, dogwood, elm, and oak

Identification: Note the broad green band as compared to the small green spots of the spiny oak-slug moth.

4681 - *Isa textula*
Crowned Slug Moth

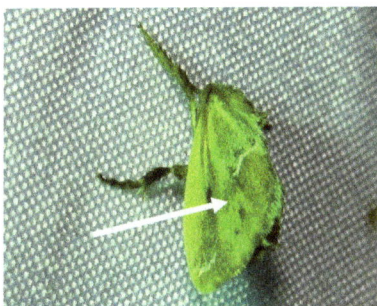

4685 - *Adoneta spinuloides*
Purple-crested Slug Moth

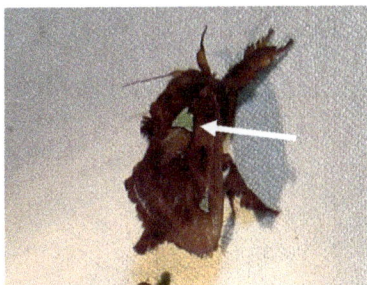

4697 - *Euclea delphinii*
Spiny Oak-slug Moth

4698 – *Parasa chloris*
Smaller Parasa Moth

4700 - *Acharia stimulea*
Saddleback Caterpillar Moth

M	A	M	J	J	A	S	O	N

Host: Several deciduous tree and shrub species.

Identification: Chocolate brown. Some have silver spots in the locations of the yellow arrows. This species also has one of the most unique looking of all caterpillars. Careful, the caterpillar's stinging cells pack quite a punch.

Epipyropidae - Planthopper Parasite Moths

As the family name implies, the caterpillars of these moths are actually an ectoparasite, living on the outside of planthoppers. Most members of the family are found in Asia.

4701 - *Fuloraecia exigua*
Planthopper Parasite Moth

M	A	M	J	J	A	S	O	N

Host: Planthoppers

Identification: This is a very small moth with wingspan frequently less than one centimeter. A bland dark moth, the males of which have very showy antennae. At Butterfly Ridge we have only found the chrysalis, which closely resembles the Sydney Opera House!

4700 – *Acharia stimulea*
Saddleback Caterpillar Moth

pupa

Photo credit: Diane Brooks

4701 - *Fuloraecia exigua*
Planthopper Parasite Moth

Crambidae - Grass Moths

This family of moths is named for their caterpillars tendency to bore into the stems of grasses to feed. These moths are normally small in size compared to more well-known moth species.

4716 - *Scoparia biplagialis*
Double-striped Scoparia Moth

| | | | | | | | | |
|M|A|M|J|J|A|S|O|N|

Host: Assumed to be grasses, not specifically known.
Identification: Small. Note the dark patches halfway down the forewing on a gray-tan background.

4738 - *Eudonia strigalis*
Striped Eudonia Moth

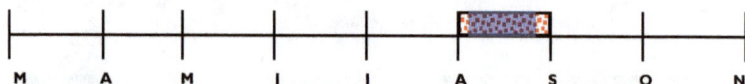

| | | | | | | | | |
|M|A|M|J|J|A|S|O|N|

Host: Assumed to be grasses, not specifically known.
Identification: This moth has dark stripes on the gray-brown forewings, similar to the 'daggers' on the wings of the Dagger Moths.

4744 - *Chrysendeton medicinalis*
Bold Medicine Moth

| | | | | | | | | |
|M|A|M|J|J|A|S|O|N|

Host: Assumed to be grasses, not specifically known.
Identification: Small. It has a very striking gold and white pattern with black spots at the trailing edge of the hindwing.

4716 – *Scoparia biplagialis*
**Double-striped Scoparia
Moth**

4738 - *Eudonia strigalis*
Striped Eudonia Moth

4744 – *Chrysendeton
medicinalis*

Bold Medicine Moth

4751 - *Elophila gyralis*
Waterlily Borer Moth

| M | A | M | J | J | A | S | O | N |

Host: Waterlily

Identification: This moth is sexually dimorphic; the male is boldly marked in brown, black, and white, while the female is a bland orange-brown. Pictured is a male. The larva are aquatic, boring into leaves and leaf stalks of Waterlily.

4826 - *Mimoschinia rufofascialis*
Rufous-banded Crambid Moth

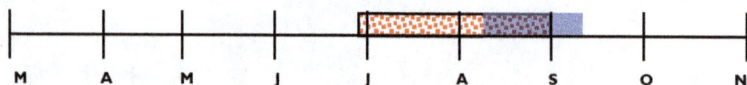

| M | A | M | J | J | A | S | O | N |

Host: Mallow

Identification: This moth is also referred to as the Barberpole Moth due to the diagonal striping on the wings.

4869 - *Glaphyria glaphyralis*
Common Glaphyria Moth

| M | A | M | J | J | A | S | O | N |

Host: Assumed to be grasses, not specifically known.

Identification: This moth is distinguished by the parallel wavy white lines on a cream-tan background. Otherwise, little is known about this species.

4751 - *Elophila gyralis*
Waterlily Borer Moth

4826 – *Mimoschinia rufofascialis*
Rufous-banded Crambid Moth

4869 - *Glaphyria glaphyralis*
Common Glaphyria Moth

4895 - *Chalcoela iphitalis*
Sooty-winged Chalcoela Moth

| | | | | | | | | |
|M|A|M|J|J|A|S|O|N|

Host: Paper wasp larva. Yes, this moth is a CARNIVORE!

Identification: The silvery frosting near the apex of the forewings makes this moth very unique in its appearance.

4945 - *Crocidophora tuberculalis*
Pale-winged Crocidiphora Moth

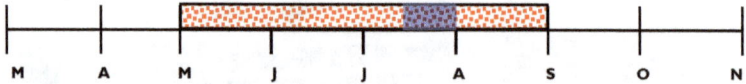

| | | | | | | | | |
|M|A|M|J|J|A|S|O|N|

Host: Assumed to be grasses, not specifically known.

Identification: This poorly marked moth looks similar to other members of the group. Males are easily distinguished by translucent marks (fovea) on the forewings.

5040 - *Pyrausta bicoloralis*
Bicolored Pyrausta Moth

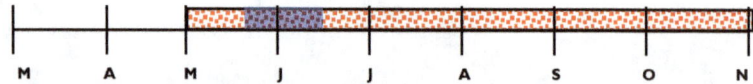

| | | | | | | | | |
|M|A|M|J|J|A|S|O|N|

Host: Assumed to be grasses, not specifically known.

Identification: This species is easily by the two-toned wings; brick red toward the apex, orange toward the body. Also note the white fringe on the wings.

5071 - *Pyrausta acrionalis*
Mint-loving Pyrausta Moth

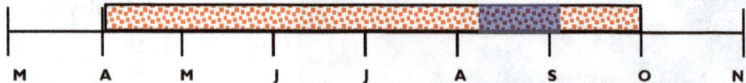

| | | | | | | | | |
|M|A|M|J|J|A|S|O|N|

Host: Mint

Identification: This moth is recognized by the red and yellow wings. Sometimes the red appears to be a mask. Looks similar to Clover Hayworm (#5524).

4895 - *Chalcoela iphitalis*
Sooty-winged Chalcoela Moth

4945 - *Crocidophora tuberculalis*
Pale-winged Crocidiphora Moth

5040 - *Pyrausta bicoloralis*
Bicolored Pyrausta Moth

5071 - *Pyrausta acrionalis*
Mint-loving Pyrausta Moth

5073 - *Pyrausta niveicilialis*
White-fringed Pyrausta Moth

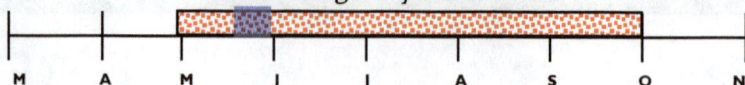

| M | A | M | J | J | A | S | O | N |

Host: Unknown

Identification: This is one of the more uniquely designed grass moths with dark forewings and a white fringe. The shape of the moth is classic grass moth, to separate it from other dark moths.

5079 - *Udea rubigalis*
Celery Leaftier Moth

| M | A | M | J | J | A | S | O | N |

Host: Celery, cabbage, cauliflower and other garden vegetables

Identification: A common garden pest. There are two circles on each forewing, the apical circle appearing to have a tail.

5143 - *Diacme adipaloides*
Darker Diacme Moth

| M | A | M | J | J | A | S | O | N |

Host: Unknown

Identification: Look for alternating orange and dark gray banding. Despite their widespread distribution, little is known about this moth.

5156 - *Nomophila nearctica*
Lucerne Moth

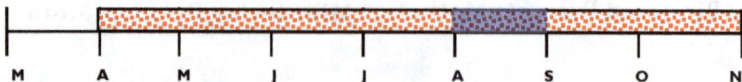

| M | A | M | J | J | A | S | O | N |

Host: Grasses and other low herbaceous plants

Identification: The two side-by-side spots on the forewing with a third toward the apex is very unique among our grass moths.

5073 - *Pyrausta niveicilialis*
White-fringed Pyrausta

5079 - *Udea rubigalis*
Celery Leaftier Moth

5143 - *Diacme adipaloides*
Darker Diacme Moth

5156 - *Nomophila nearctica*
Lucerne Moth

5159 - *Desmia funeralis*
Grape Leaffolder Moth

| M | A | M | J | J | A | S | O | N |

Host: Grape and Virginia creeper
Identification: The three obvious white spots on each side make this bug obvious. There is also a white stripe on the abdomen. One of the most frequently encountered moths at Butterfly Ridge.

5169 - *Hymenia perspectalis*
Spotted Beet Webworm Moth

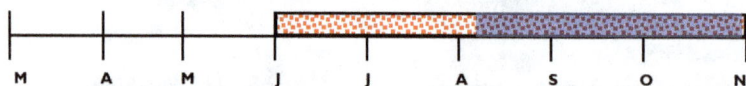

| M | A | M | J | J | A | S | O | N |

Host: Beets, chard, and potatoes
Identification: This moth has fewer white lines on the wings than the very similar next species.

5172 - *Diasemiodes janassialis*

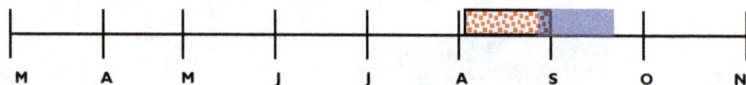

| M | A | M | J | J | A | S | O | N |

Host: Unknown
Identification: The submarginal white line on the forewing goes nearly completely across the wing while the previous webworm's line goes only a fraction of the distance. Also, this species has two obvious white hindwing lines, while the webworm has only one.

5175 - *Diathrausta harlequinalis*
Harlequin Webworm Moth

| M | A | M | J | J | A | S | O | N |

Host: Unknown
Identification: This moth is very similar to *Diasemiodes* except that the lines on the wings are orange rather than white.

88

5159 - *Desmia funeralis*
Grape Leaffolder Moth

5169 - *Hymenia perspectalis*
Spotted Beet Webworm Moth

5172 - *Diasemiodes janassialis*

5175 - *Diathrausta harlequinalis*
Harlequin Webworm Moth

5176 - *Anageshna primordialis*
Yellow-spotted Webworm Moth

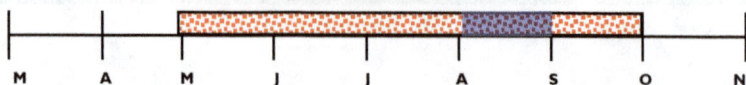

M A M J J A S O N

Host: Unknown

Identification: This moth is very similar to several species on the previous page. The markings on the wings however have a definitely yellow tinge, rather than white. Little is known about the species.

5182 - *Blepharomastix ranalis*
Hollow-spotted Blepharomastix Moth

M A M J J A S O N

Host: Lamb's quarters

Identification: White with the black striping is unique among our southeast Ohio moths. The "hollow spots" are noted by the black arrows.

5223 - *Palpita illibalis*
Inkblot Palpita Moth

M A M J J A S O N

Host: Unknown

Identification: This moth has fewer dark markings than its cousin the Splendid Palpita.

5226 - *Palpita magniferalis*
Splendid Palpita Moth

M A M J J A S O N

Host: Ash

Identification: Splendid Palpita has many more dark markings on the silvery background than its close cousin the Inkblot Palpita.

5176 - *Anageshna primordialis*
Yellow-spotted Webworm Moth

5182 - *Blepharomastix ranalis*
Hollow-spotted Blepharomastix Moth

5223 – *Palpita illibalis*
Inkblot Palpita Moth

5226 - *Palpita magniferalis*
Splendid Palpita Moth

5228 - *Polygrammodes flavidales*
Ironweed Root Moth

| M | A | M | J | J | A | S | O | N |

Host: Ironweed

Identification: Small with a series of thin red lines on a cream-colored background.

5241 - *Pantographa limata*
Basswood Leafroller Moth

| M | A | M | J | J | A | S | O | N |

Host: Basswood and oak

Identification: The hindwings have a sort of purplish, mother-of-pearl look when exposed to light.

5255 - *Diastictis ventralis*
White-spotted Brown Moth

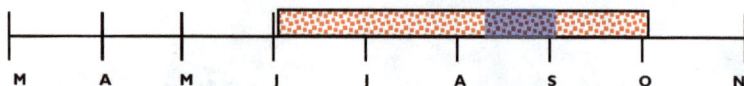

| M | A | M | J | J | A | S | O | N |

Host: Unknown

Identification: The small white spots on the dark background is unique among the grass moths. Very little is known about this species.

5276 - *Herpetogramma abdominalis*

| M | A | M | J | J | A | S | O | N |

Host: Nettle

Identification: This moth looks very much like the Zigzag Herpetogramma moth except that the marginal shading on the forewings is much lighter than on the Zigzag.

5228 - *Polygrammodes flavidales*
Ironweed Root Moth

5241 – *Pantographa limata*
Basswood Leafroller Moth

5255 - *Diastictis ventralis*
White-spotted Brown Moth

5276 - *Herpetogramma abdominalis*

5277 - *Herpetogramma thestealis*
Zigzag Herpetogramma Moth

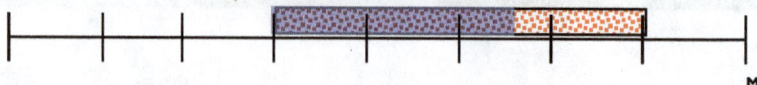

Host: Basswood

Identification: The dark loops on this moth almost gives it the appearance of bird wings. The dark shading on the wing margin distinguishes this species from the previous.

5279.1 - *Herpetogramma sphingealis*
Christmas Fern Moth

M A M J J A S O N

Host: Christmas fern

Identification: This moth is recognized by the dark, shimmering wings with lone light spot near upper wing margin. Very little is known about this moth.

5280 - *Herpetogramma aeglealis*
Septentine Webworm Moth

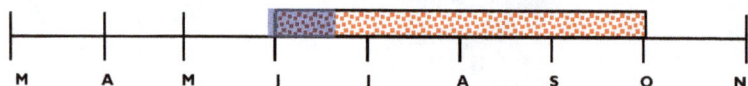

M A M J J A S O N

Host: Ferns

Identification: Perhaps the best way to describe this moth is an intermediate between zigzag moth and Christmas fern moth

5292 - *Conchylodes ovulalis*
Zebra Conchylodes Moth

M A M J J A S O N

Host: Several members of the Sunflower Family

Identification: Black striping on a white background. This species is similar in appearance to the hollow-spotted blepharomastix (Hodge's #5182), however the conchylodes has more black stripes as well as prominent black stripes on the abdomen.

5277 – *Herpetogramma thestealis*
Zigzag Herpetogramma Moth

5279.1 – *Herpetogramma sphingealis*
Christmas Fern Moth

5280 - *Herpetogramma aeglealis*
Septentine Webworm Moth

5292 – *Conchylodes ovulalis*
Zebra Conchylodes Moth

5362 - *Crambus agitatellus*
Double-banded Grass-veneer Moth

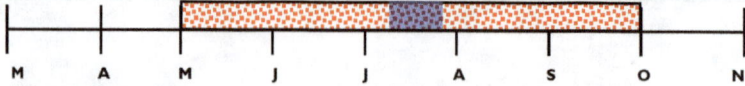

| M | A | M | J | J | A | S | O | N |

Host: Grasses

Identification: The broad white strip on the forewing of this moth is interrupted by a thin orange-brown line.

5403 - *Agriphila vulgivagellus*
Vagabond Crambus Moth

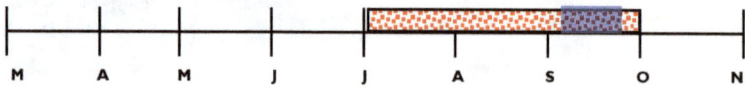

| M | A | M | J | J | A | S | O | N |

Host: Grasses

Identification: The pattern on this moth is very unique among our grass moths with the wing veins being a solid pale color with a grainy-looking gray between the veins. This moth is an agricultural pest in some areas.

5419 - *Microcrambus biguttellus*
Gold-stripe Grass-veneer Moth

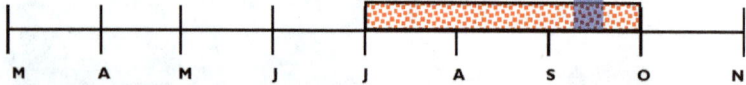

| M | A | M | J | J | A | S | O | N |

Host: Probably grasses

Identification: Normally two small black spots on a white background are the only features you can make out on this very small moth.

5420 - *Microcrambus elegans*
Elegant Grass-veneer Moth

| M | A | M | J | J | A | S | O | N |

Host: Grasses

Identification: The pattern of gold, white, and dark is very distinctive in this very small moth. The most abundant of the grass moths at Butterfly Ridge.

5362 - *Crambus agitatellus*
Double-banded Grass-veneer Moth

5403 - *Agriphila vulgivagellus*
Vagabond Crambus Moth

5419 – *Microcrambus biguttellus*
Gold-stripe Grass-veneer Moth

5420 – *Microcrambus elegans*
Elegant Grass-veneer Moth

5450 - *Parapediasia decorellus*
Graceful Grass-veneer Moth

| M | A | M | J | J | A | S | O | N |

Host: Probably grasses

Identification: This moth is recognized by its graying color with an orange forewing fringe. Within the orange margin are black dots.

5451 - *Parapediasia decorellus*
Bluegrass Webworm Moth

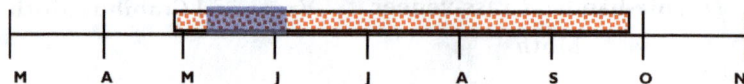

| M | A | M | J | J | A | S | O | N |

Host: Bluegrass

Identification: This moth is similar in appearance as other grass-veneer moths. Light gray or tan in color with a dark gray smudge on the 'rolled' forewings.

5464 - *Urola nivalis*
Snowy Urola Moth

| M | A | M | J | J | A | S | O | N |

Host: Grasses

Identification: This moth has satiny white wings with a gold fringe on the forewings. Easily recognized among our smaller moths.

5450 – *Parapediasia decorellus*
Graceful Grass-veneer Moth

5451 – *Parapediasia teterrella*
Bluegrass Webworm Moth

5464 – *Urola nivalis*
Snowy Urola Moth

Pyralidae - Snout Moths

This family of moths is named for their narrow heads that appear to protrude beyond the point of wing attachment. Some members of this family are known to be crop pests.

5518 - *Aglossa cuprina*
Grease Moth

Host: Grain

Identification: A very odd wing pattern to describe. Look for the large 'tooth' design on each forewing. Considered a pest in stored grains.

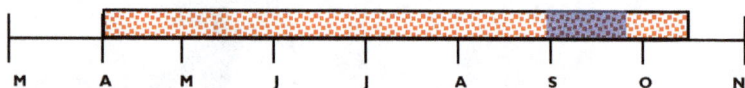

5524 - *Hypsopygia costalis*
Clover Hayworm Moth

Host: Dried plant material

Identification: This moth has a pair of large yellow edge spots on a maroon background with a yellow marginal fringe.

5530 - *Hypsopygia binodulalis*
Pink-fringed Dolichomia Moth

Host: Unknown

Identification: Much like clover hayworm but paler and with obvious lines extending from yellow spots across wings. Very little is known about this moth.

5518 - *Aglossa cuprina*
Grease Moth

5524 - *Hypsopygia costalis*
Clover Hayworm

5530 – *Hypsopygia binodulalis*
Pink-fringed Dolichomia Moth

5552 - *Galasa nigrinodis*
Boxwood Leaftier Moth

| M | A | M | J | J | A | S | O | N |

Host: Boxwood

Identification: This species is easily recognized by it's "push-up" posture and by the indentations in the forewings.

5556 - *Tosale oviplagalis*
Dimorphic Tosale Moth

| M | A | M | J | J | A | S | O | N |

Host: Unknown

Identification: This species is sexually dimorphic. In this case, the two sexes share the same pattern but males are brown and females are gray. Pictured is a male.

5571 - *Condylolomia participalis*
Drab Condylolomia Moth

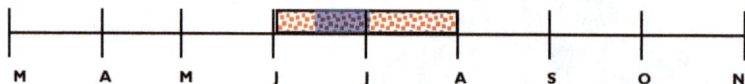

| M | A | M | J | J | A | S | O | N |

Host: Unknown

Identification: The common name for this moth is certainly fitting. Some individuals have 'growths' on the leading edge of the forewing, but not all have this. The moth pictured does not have the growth, with the arrow indicating where the growth would be. Preferred habitat for this species is bogs and swamps.

5552 – *Galasa nigrinodis*
Boxwood Leaftier Moth

5556 - *Tosale oviplagalis*
Dimorphic Tosale Moth

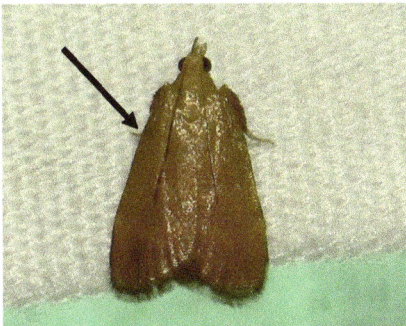

5571 - *Condylolomia
participalis*
Drab Condylolomia Moth

5577 - *Epipaschia superatalis*
Dimorphic Macalla Moth

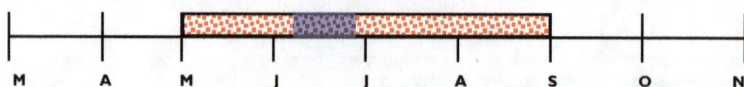

| M | A | M | J | J | A | S | O | N |

Host: Poison ivy and possibly sumacs.

Identification: Easily recognized by the two-toned color, with rust color toward the wing apex and gray-green closer to the body. This also one of the few poison ivy feeders, which we could always use more of!

5588 - *Oneida lunulalis*
Orange-tufted Oneida Moth

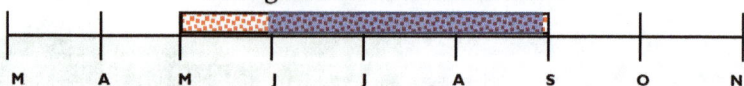

| M | A | M | J | J | A | S | O | N |

Host: Oak

Identification: The identifying feature that stands out on this species is the dark, circular spot near the wing apex against a gray-silver background.

5595 - *Pococera robustella*
Pine Webworm Moth

| M | A | M | J | J | A | S | O | N |

Host: Pine

Identification: The *Pococera* moths all have a very similar appearance, with the wings divided into three color schemes. The third nearest the body normally has a black line that separates this section form the middle section (see any of the other Pococeras). Pine Webworm however does not have the line that separate the two sections which makes it unique among this group of moths. The pupa of this species pupates in the soil beneath the pine tree host.

5577 - *Epipaschia superatalis*
Dimorphic Macalla Moth

5588 - *Oneida lunulalis*
Orange-tufted Oneida

5595 - *Pococera robustella*
Pine Webworm Moth

5603 - *Pococera maritimalis*

| M | A | M | J | J | A | S | O | N |

Host: Unknown

Identification: The color scheme of this *Pococera* from the top down is tan/gray/rust. Also note the subtle circular patterns on each hindwing and the subtle metallic margin near the apex.

5604 - *Pococera militella*
Sycamore Webworm Moth

| M | A | M | J | J | A | S | O | N |

Host: Unknown

Identification: The color scheme of this *Pococera* from the top down is orange-brown/tan/tan. The upper orange-brown section of each forewing also has a small dark line resembling an eye brow.

5606 - *Pococera asperatella*
Maple Webworm Moth

| M | A | M | J | J | A | S | O | N |

Host: Maple, oak, and beech

Identification: Many of the webworm moths have a dark line that runs perpendicular across the forewing. Maple webworm has what looks sort of like a mask with white eyebrows, the dark line mentioned previously forming the upper edge of the mask..

5608 - *Pococera expandens*
Striped Oak Webworm Moth

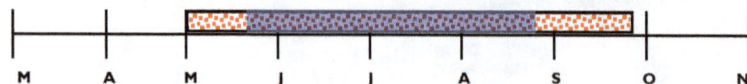

| M | A | M | J | J | A | S | O | N |

Host: Oak

Identification: The golden forward half contrasting with the dark back half is unique among these small moths. Little is known about this species.

5603 - *Pococera maritimalis*

5604 - *Pococera militella*
Sycamore Webworm Moth

5606 – *Pococera asperatella*
Maple Webworm Moth

5608 – *Pococera expandens*
Striped Oak Webworm Moth

5674 - *Acrobasis demotella*
Walnut Shoot Moth

Host: Walnut and hickory

Identification: This moth is similar to the *Pococera* moths with the wings divided into three color schemes. The color scheme for this moth from top to bottom is brown/black/rust with each segment separated by a white line.

5775.2 - *Salebriaria rufimacalatella*
White-banded Salebriaria

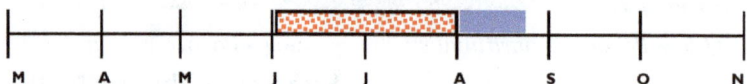

Host: Oak

Identification: This moth is easily recognized by the red blush above the white forewing band. There is also a dark, zigzag line through the white band.

5794 - *Sciota vetustella*

Host: Unknown

Identification: This moth is easily recognized by the rust-colored upper half of the forewings. Apparently very little is known about this species.

5796 - *Sciota subcaesiella*
Locust Leafroller Moth

Host: Locust and wisteria

Identification: This moth has a white zigzag through the middle of the forewing with black just above. There is also a reddish tint throughout the moth.

5674 - *Acrobasis demotella*
Walnut Shoot Moth

5775.2 - *Salebrairia rufimacalatella*
White-banded Salebrairia

5794 – *Sciota vetustella*

5796 - *Sciota subcaesiella*
Locust Leafroller Moth

5861.1 - *Dioryctria resinosella*
Red Pine Shoot Moth

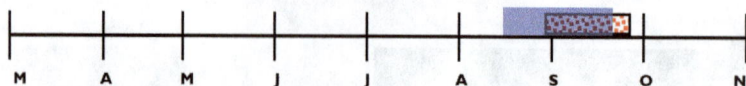

M   A   M   J   J   A   S   O   N

Host: Red pine

Identification: There are several pine shoot borers that look very similar and none of which are common in Ohio. This species has two white zigzag lines with white frosting on the inside edge of the lines.

5999 - *Eulogia ochrifrontella*
Broad-banded Eulogia Moth

M   A   M   J   J   A   S   O   N

Host: Unknown

Identification: One of those little brown moths that will drive you nuts trying to identify! Note dark band across the middle. A white line separates the dark band on each side.

6001 - *Ephestiodes infimella*
Reddish Ephestiodes Moth

M   A   M   J   J   A   S   O   N

Host: Unknown

Identification: The front half of this moth is cream-pumpkin color. The rest of the moth is dark but with a reddish tint throughout.

6029 - *Varneria postremella*

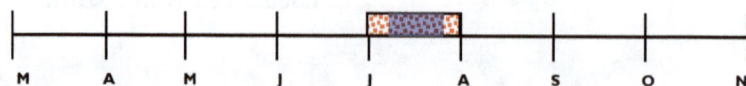

M   A   M   J   J   A   S   O   N

Host: Unknown

Identification: This is a very small moth that is a solid brick red color.

5861.1 – *Dioryctria resinosella*
Red Pine Shoot Moth

5999 - *Eulogia ochrifrontella*
**Broad-banded
Eulogia Moth**

6001 - *Ephestiodes infimella*
Reddish Ephestiodes Moth

6029 - *Varneria postremella*

6053 - *Peoria approximella*
Carmine Snout Moth

| M | A | M | J | J | A | S | O | N |

Host: Unknown

Identification: The red wash on the white background is unique for our local small moths. Very little is known about this species.

Thyrididae - Picture-wing Leaf Moths

The Picture-wing Leaf Moths are a small group of moths, a total of four species in Ohio, that tend to have boldly-marked wings and fly during the day.

6076 - *Thyris maculata*
Spotted Thyris Moth

| M | A | M | J | J | A | S | O | N |

Host: Clematis and bluets

Identification: The white spots and orange near the forewing point of attachment are the characters to look for on this moth. It flies during the day and has white wing margins that make the wings look sharply angled.

Pterophoridae - Plume Moths

The Plume Moths are known for having very feathery looking wings. At rest, the wings actually fold-up, much like an Oriental fan, and look very narrow.

6053 - Peoria approximella
Carmine Snout Moth

6076 – Thyris maculata
Spotted Thyris Moth

6091 - *Geina periscelidactylus*
Grape Plume Moth

M   A   M   J   J   A   S   O   N

Host: Grape and Virginia creeper

Identification: There are several plume moths found in Ohio. The grape plume is recognized by the brown brand on the tan base-colored forewings.

6093 - *Geina buscki*

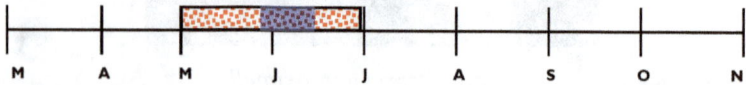

M   A   M   J   J   A   S   O   N

Host: Unknown

Identification: Our darkest plume moth, with bold contrasting chocolate brown and white wings. The legs are brown and white striped.

6109 - *Platyptilia carduidactylus*
Artichoke Plume Moth

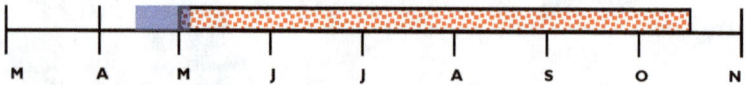

M   A   M   J   J   A   S   O   N

Host: Thistle

Identification: There are several plume moths found in Ohio. The artichoke plume is recognized by the brown triangle in the forewings.

6160 - *Adaina ambrosiae*
Ambrosia Plume Moth

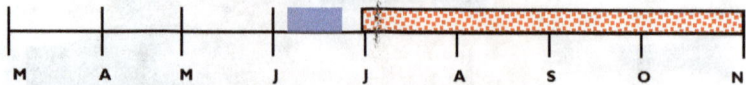

M   A   M   J   J   A   S   O   N

Host: Thistle

Identification: This plume moth is easily recognized by its pale color with dark marginal spots.

6091 – *Geina periscelidactylus*
Grape Plume Moth

6093 – Geina biscki

6109 – *Platyptilia carduidactylus*
Artichoke Plume Moth

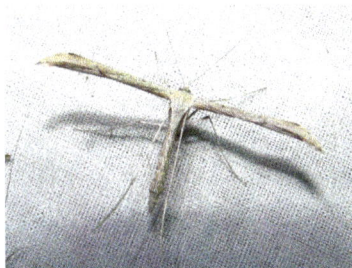

6160 - *Adaina ambrosiae*
Ambrosia Plume Moth

6213 - *Hellinsia lacteodactylus*

| M | A | M | J | J | A | S | O | N |

Host: Goldenrod and boneset

Identification: This is a very pale plume moth. The interior two -thirds of the forewing is 'dirty' compared to the apical third. It also has a small gray dot on each wing that is sometimes visible.

6226 - *Hellinsia unicolor*

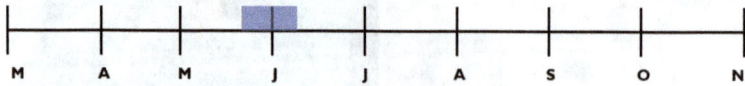

| M | A | M | J | J | A | S | O | N |

Host: Unknown

Identification: Another very pale plume moth but the color is more consistent than *H. lacteodactylus*. This species also lacks the gray spot on the forewing. Very little is known about this moth.

6234 - *Emmelina monodactyla*
Morning Glory Plume Moth

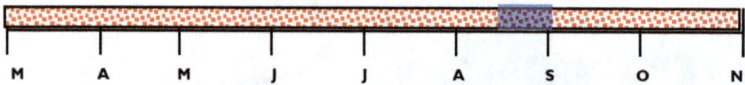

| M | A | M | J | J | A | S | O | N |

Host: Morning Glory

Identification: Another pale plume moth, similar in appearance to *H. unicolor* but perhaps more grayish. The body is rather ornate with several parallel toothed stripes.

6213 - *Hellinsia lacteodactylus*

6226 - *Hellinsia unicolor*

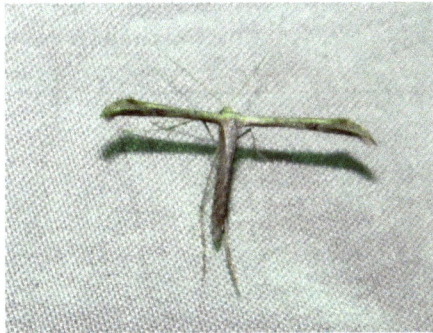

6234 - *Emmelina monodactyla*
Morning Glory Plume Moth

Drepanoidae - Hook-tip Moths

Many, but not all, members of this moth family have distinctive hooks at the tips of their forewings.

....

6237 - *Pseudothyatira cymatophoroides*
Tufted Thyatirid Moth

Host: Alder, birch, maple, oak and others

Identification: Butterfly Ridge has two different forms of this moth. The collar near the point of attachement of the hindwings as well as a dark spot near the lower apical corner are distinctive to this moth.

....

6240 - *Euthyatira pudens*
Dogwood Thyatirid Moth

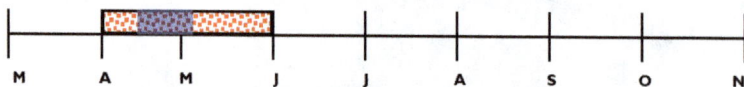

Host: Flowering dogwood (*Cornus florida*)

Identification: This species is easily recognized by the three distinct white/pink spots on the forewing.

....

6251 - *Drepana arcuata*
Arched Hooktip Moth

Host: Alder and birch

Identification: The hooked wing tips are a dead giveaway for this moth. A common summer visitor at the Butterfly Ridge moth sheet!

6237 - *Pseudothyatira
cymatophoroides*
Form: typical
Tufted Thyatirid Moth

6237 - *Pseudothyatira
cymatophoroides*
Form: expultrix
Tufted Thyatirid Moth

6240 – *Euthyatira pudens*
Dogwood Thyatirid Moth

6251 - *Drepana arcuata*
Arched Hooktip

Geometridae - Inch-worm Moths

As children, many of us referred to the caterpillars of this family of moths as inch-worms. Many of the adults have "angled" wings, looking as if they were trimmed with pinking shears.

6261 - *Heliomata cycladata*
Common Spring Moth

| M | A | M | J | J | A | S | O | N |

Host: Black locust and honeylocust

Identification: The large white hindwing spot is unlike any other small moth that we have. These moths can be found both day and night.

6271.1 - *Mellilla xanthometata*
Orangewing Moth

| M | A | M | J | J | A | S | O | N |

Host: Black locust

Identification: The solid orange hindwing is very distinctive for this moth and they frequently display the hindwing. The phenology bars above reflect that there are two generations per year.

6273 - *Speranza pustularia*
Lesser Maple Spanworm Moth

| M | A | M | J | J | A | S | O | N |

Host: Maple, birch, and cherry

Identification: The plain white background with cinnamon-colored stripes is unique among our summer moths. The most common moth at the Butterfly Ridge sheet in the summer!

6261 - *Heliomata cycladata*
Common Spring Moth

6271.1 - *Mellilla xanthometata*
Orangewing Moth

6273 – *Speranza pustularia*
Lesser Maple Spanworm Moth

Macaria sp. - Angle Moths

It can be very difficult to tell the different species of *Macaria* apart. As example, the distinguishing feature that sets apart *M. promiscuata* is a swelling of the shin on the rear legs! In Ohio all of the *Macaria* that we have observed at Butterfly Ridge have the same general flight season.

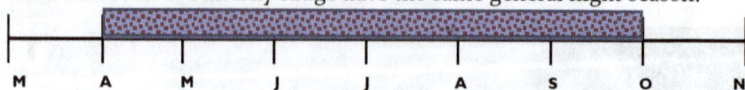

M	A	M	J	J	A	S	O	N

6326 - *Macaria aemulataria*
Common Angle Moth

Host: Maple

Identification: A smaller, lighter version of promiscuous angle.

6331 - *Macaria promiscuata*
Promiscuous Angle Moth

Host: Maple and locust

Identification: Note dark forewing spot and dark lining on forewing notch.

6339 - *Macaria transitaria*
Blurry Chocolate Angle Moth

Host: Pine

Identification: Note yellow head and chocolate band near the margin of each wing.

6340 - *Macaria minorata*
Minor Angle Moth

Host: Pine

Identification: Note yellow head. The dark lines on the forewings are more prominent than on chocolate angle.

6341 - *Macaria bicolorata*
Bicolored Angle Moth

Host: Pine

Identification: Much like the others on this page, having gold head and prominent forewing lines. Hindwings have obvious two-tone coloration.

6326 – *Macaria aemulatari*
Common Angle Moth

6331 - *Macaria promiscuata*
Promiscuous Angle

6339– *Macaria transitaria*
Blurry Chocolate Angle Moth

6340 - *Macaria minorata*
Minor Angle Moth

6341 – *Macaria bicolorata*
Bicolored Angle Moth

6344 - *Macaria signaria*
Pale-marked Angle Moth

Host: Several species of coniferous trees

Identification: Wing base color more brown than Hemlock Angle. No notch lining. Dark bands/lines on forewing more prominent than on Hemlock.

6348 - *Macaria fissinotata*
Hemlock Angle Moth

Host: Hemlock

Identification: General gray color (not brown). No notch lining. Forewing bands/lines prominent only at the leading margin.

6352 - *Macaria granitata*
Granite Moth

Host: Scrub pine

Identification: White/dark gray marbling on forewing makes this one of the few easy to identify *Macarias*.

6344 - *Macaria signaria*
Pale-marked Angle Moth

6348 - *Macaria fissinotata*
Hemlock Angle

6352 – *Macaria granitata*
Granite Moth

6386 - *Digrammia ocellinata*
Faint-spotted Angle Moth

| M | A | M | J | J | A | S | O | N |

Host: Black locust and honeylocust

Identification: The dark band near the wing margin with the absence of the apical notch distinguishes this moth from other Angles.

6430 - *Orthofidonia flavivenata*
Yellow-veined Geometer Moth

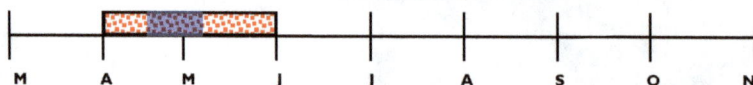

| M | A | M | J | J | A | S | O | N |

Host: Unknown

Identification: The yellow veins in the wings are unique among Ohio moths.

6586 - *Iridopsis defectaria*
Brown-shaded Gray Moth

| M | A | M | J | J | A | S | O | N |

Host: Oak, poplar, willow, and cherry

Identification: Rather than having the bold lines of the bent-line gray, this species has brown bands. Also note the thin-lined circles on the hindwings indicated by circles.

6588 - *Iridopsis larvaria*
Bent-line Moth

| M | A | M | J | J | A | S | O | N |

Host: Several deciduous tree species

Identification: Look for the bold, rounded lines on the wings.

6386 - *Digrammia ocellinata*
Faint-spotted Angle Moth

6430 – *Orthofidonia flavivenata*
**Yellow-veined Geometer
Moth**

6586 - *Iridopsis defectaria*
Brown-shaded Gray

6588 - *Iridopsis larvaria*
Bent-line Gray

6590 - *Anavitrinella pampinaria*
Common Gray Moth

M   A   M   J   J   A   S   O   N

Host: Apple, pear, ash, elm, poplar and willow

Identification: The horizontal shading from the forewing apex toward the body is distinctive for this species. This moth is found throughout all of North America.

6594 - *Cleora sublunaria*
Double-lined Gray Moth

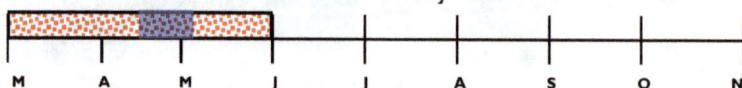

M   A   M   J   J   A   S   O   N

Host: Oak

Identification: The 'collar' of this species is comprised of two separate lines, hence the name 'double-lined'.

6597 - *Ectropis crepuscularia*
Small Engrailed Moth

M   A   M   J   J   A   S   O   N

Host: Several deciduous tree species

Identification: This species has distinctive shading under the lateral lines on the wings and frequently sports a white head. Supposedly this species has one generation in the north but our data refutes that.

6599 - *Epimecis hortaria*
Tuliptree Beauty Moth

M   A   M   J   J   A   S   O   N

Host: Tuliptree, pawpaw, sassafras, and poplar

Identification: Looks like a lot of other geometrids! Resembles the Gray Moths but with more subtle, jagged lines and bold banding. This is also one of our largest geometrids with a wing-span of two inches.

6590 - *Anavitrinella pampinaria*
Common Gray Moth

6594 - *Cleora sublunaria*
Double-lined Gray Moth

6597 - *Ectropis crepuscularia*
Small Engrailed Moth

6599 - *Epimecis hortaria*
Tulip-tree Beauty Moth

6620 - *Melanolophia canadaria*
Canadian Melanolophia Moth

M   A   M   J   J   A   S   O   N

Host: Pine, oak, maple, and several others.

Identification: Unfortunately this non-descript moth can be easily confused with worn versions of several geometrids. Look for four rows of toothed lines and the dark spot near the apex seems to be one of the few consistent features of this moth.

6638 - *Eufidonia notataria*
Powder Moth

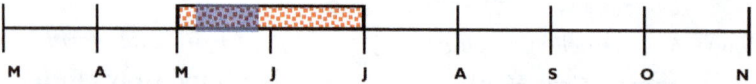

M   A   M   J   J   A   S   O   N

Host: Unknown

Identification: The white base color with dark blotches is unique and gives this moth more of a Checkered-Skipper butterfly look. Varies greatly in appearance. The appearance of this moth at our sheet was a huge surprise, considering it's the only documented sighting of this moth from southeast Ohio. This could possibly be *Eufidonia discospilata*, but genitalia inspection is required to distinguish between the two. In addition, the habitat for E. discospilata is described as bogs and barrens, which are absent from our site.

6640 - *Biston betularia*
Peppered Moth

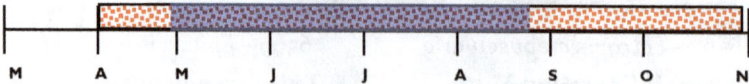

M   A   M   J   J   A   S   O   N

Host: A wide variety of plants

Identification: This moth is sort of a salt and pepper color with dark veins in the wing. Another unique characteristic about the Peppered Moth is the way it holds its wings. The forewings are held lower, nearly completely concealing the hindwings.

6620 – *Melanolophia canadaria*
**Canadian Melanolophia
Moth**

6638 - *Eufidonia notataria*
Powder Moth

6640 - *Biston betularia*
Peppered Moth

6654 - *Hypagyrtis unipunctata*
One-spotted Variant Moth

M   A   M   J   J   A   S   O   N

Host: Many species of deciduous trees plus pine.

Identification: The One-spotted Variant is one of the most variable of our moths, coming in a variety of colors and markings. The one thing that is consistent is the white spot near the apex of each forewing.

....

6655 - *Hypagyrtis esther*
Esther Moth

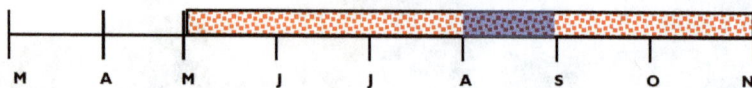

M   A   M   J   J   A   S   O   N

Host: Pine.

Identification: The Esther Moth is very similar to the one-spotted variant in appearance. The colors of the Esther Moth are normally more consistent. Plus the colors on one-spotted variant tend to be mottled, not a smooth, solid color as in Esther.

6654 - *Hypagyrtis unipunctata*
One-spotted Variant Moth

6655 - *Hypagyrtis esther*
Esther Moth

6659 - *Phigalia denticulata*
Toothed Phigalia Moth

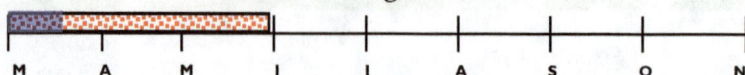

| M | A | M | J | J | A | S | O | N |

Host: Unknown

Identification: The toothed phigalia is much like the peppered moth in holding its forewings low, however wingshape is different. In addition, two of the dark lines nearly come together at the lower margin of the wing, unlike the peppered moth. This is one of our earliest fliers in the spring.

6667 - *Lomographa vestaliata*
White Spring Moth

| M | A | M | J | J | A | S | O | N |

Host: Many species of deciduous trees

Identification: This a moderately small moth with translucent white wings. Reports are that this species has one generation per year, but our data suggests otherwise.

Euchlaena sp. - Euchlaena Moths

The Euchlaena's as a group are one of the easier to identify among the Inch-worm Moths due to the very jagged margins of the hindwings.

6726 - *Euchlaena obtusaria*
Obtuse Euchlaena

| M | A | M | J | J | A | S | O | N |

Host: Rose and impatiens

Identification: Perhaps the most drably marked of the Euchlaenas. The deeply 'pinked' hindwings and the dark apical spot on the forewings is key to the identification of this moth.

659 – *Phigalia denticulata*
Toothed Phigalia Moth

6667 – *Lomographa vestiliata*
White Spring Moth

6726 – *Euchlaena obtusaria*
Obtuse Euchlaena Moth

6733 - *Euchlaena amoenaria*
Deep Yellow Euchlaena

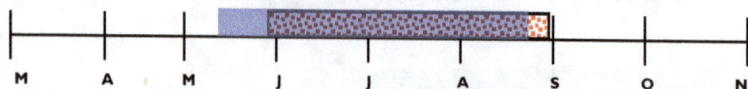

M	A	M	J	J	A	S	O	N

Host: Unknown

Identification: This *Euchlaena* is easily recognized by the dark marginal bands and the light apical spot within the dark marginal band of the forewing.

6735 - *Euchlaena pectinaria*
Forked Euchlaena

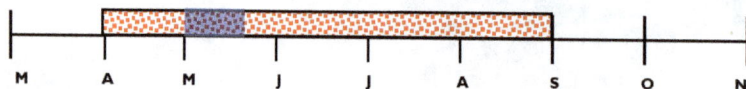

M	A	M	J	J	A	S	O	N

Host: Unknown

Identification: This Euchlaena has red spotting throughout with a more solid red band toward the margins. The light apical spot that is so prominent in the Deep yellow euchlaena is much more subtle in forked euchlaena.

6737 - *Euchlaena tigrinaria*
Mottled Euchlaena

M	A	M	J	J	A	S	O	N

Host: Poplar, birch, dogwood, and hazelnut

Identification: Easily recognized from the other euchlaenas at Butterfly Ridge by the "mottled" bands rather than solid bands.

6733 - *Euchlaena amoenaria*
Deep Yellow Euchlaena

6735 - *Euchlaena pectinaria*
Forked Euchlaena

6737 – *Euchlaena tigrinaria*
Mottled Euchlaena Moth

6740 - *Xanthotype urticaria*
False Crocus Geometer Moth

| | | | | | | | | |
|M|A|M|J|J|A|S|O|N|

Host: Dogwood and goldenrod

Identification: The yellow wings with red blotches is quite unique among geometers. There is debate whether this moth and the next one are in fact separate species or the same bug.

6743 - *Xanthotype sospeta*
Crocus Geometer Moth

| | | | | | | | | |
|M|A|M|J|J|A|S|O|N|

Host: Willow, dogwood, viburnum

Identification: Some consider this species and false crocus to be the same. In my experience, the false crocus has much more red spotting.

6748 - *Pero ancetaria*
Hubner's Pero Moth

| | | | | | | | | |
|M|A|M|J|J|A|S|O|N|

Host: Alder, back cherry, and willow

Identification: This moth is unmistakable with the undulating margin between brown and yellow on the forewings.

6763 - *Phaeoura quernaria*
Oak Beauty Moth

| | | | | | | | | |
|M|A|M|J|J|A|S|O|N|

Host: Oak and several other deciduous trees

Identification: The overall color of this moth varies from brown to nearly black with consistent, conspicuous white spots on the leading forewing margin.

6740 - *Xanthotype urticaria*
False Crocus Geometer Moth

6743 - *Xanthotype sospeta*
Crocus Geometer Moth

6748 - *Pero ancetaria*
Hubner's Pero Moth

6763 – *Phaeoura quernaria*
Oak Beauty Moth

6796 - *Campaea perlata*
Pale Beauty Moth

M	A	M	J	J	A	S	O	N

Host: Several deciduous trees

Identification: This moth has the jagged margin of the hindwing much like a euchlaena, but is white. The narrow bands in the middle of the wings distinguish this from snowy geometer (Hodge's #6965).

6797 - *Ennomos magnaria*
Maple Spanworm Moth

M	A	M	J	J	A	S	O	N

Host: Several species of deciduous trees

Identification: The strongly-angled, pinked nature of the wing margins is unique, even among the geometrids.

6818 - *Selenia kentaria*
Kent's Geometer

M	A	M	J	J	A	S	O	N

Host: Cherry and birch

Identification: This moth frequently folds it's wings over its back, much like a butterfly. Look for the silvery 'comma' on the underside of the hindwing.

6823 - *Metarranthis angularia*
Angled Metarranthis Moth

M	A	M	J	J	A	S	O	N

Host: Cherry

Identification: You will recognize this moth by the alternating dark- and light-colored bands

6796 - *Campaea perlata*
Pale Beauty

6797 - *Ennomos magnaria*
Maple Spanworm Moth

6818 - *Selenia kentaria*
Kent's Geometer

6823 - *Metarranthis angularia*
Angled Metarranthis Moth

6828 - *Metarranthis homuraria*
Purplish Metarranthis Moth

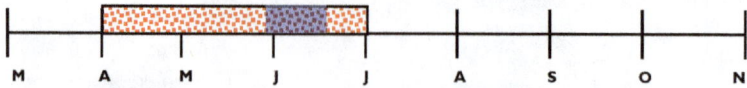

| M | A | M | J | J | A | S | O | N |

Host: Unknown

Identification: On the purplish metarranthis, the dark medial band comes to a sharp point, whereas on angled metarranthis that band is more rounded. Otherwise, little is known about this moth.

6838 - *Probole amicaria*
Friendly Probole Moth

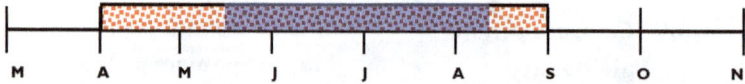

| M | A | M | J | J | A | S | O | N |

Host: Sourwood

Identification: There are several relatively large speckled geometers. The friendly probole is recognized by the large tooth that extends nearly to the margin.

Plagodis sp. - Plagodis Moths

The Plagodis Moths are among the most beautiful of Butterfly Ridge's moths. They are small, not much larger than your thumbnail, but very striking in appearance. Many of them feature a very bold "wood grain" look. In addition, the squared-off apexes of the forewings are unique.

6836 - *Plagodis pulveraria*
American Barred Umber Moth

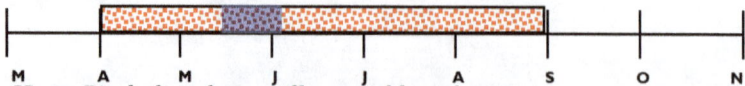

| M | A | M | J | J | A | S | O | N |

Host: Birch, hazelnut, willow, and hawthorn

Identification: The base color is a sort of a wood grain tan look with what looks like dark 'Batman' wings in the middle of the forewings.

6828 - *Metarranthis*
homuraria
**Purplish Metarranthis
Moth**

6838 - *Probole amicaria*
Friendly Probole Moth

6836 - *Plagodis pulveraria*
**American Barred
Umber Moth**

6840 - *Plagodis serinaria*
Lemon Plagodis Moth

M   A   M   J   J   A   S   O   N

Host: Poplar, birch, and cherry
Identification: Lemon yellow with a burgundy blush.   A beautiful moth!

6841 - *Plagodis kuetzingi*
Purple Plagodis Moth

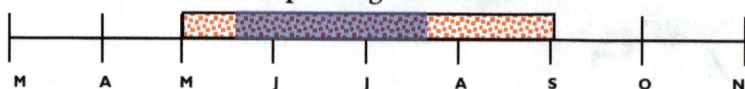

M   A   M   J   J   A   S   O   N

Host: Ash
Identification: The apical half of all wings are dark purple.

6842 - *Plagodis phlogosaria*
Straight-lined Plagodis Moth

M   A   M   J   J   A   S   O   N

Host: Willow, birch, and cherry
Identification: Distinct dark lines on a wood-grain background.

6843 - *Plagodis fervidaria*
Fervid Plagodis Moth

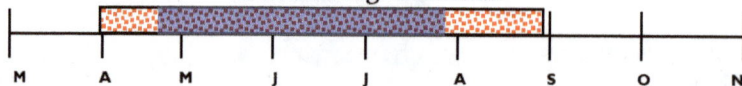

M   A   M   J   J   A   S   O   N

Host: Several deciduous tree species
Identification: Wood grain throughout with darker bands.

6844 - *Plagodis alcoolaria*
Hollow-spotted Plagodis Moth

M   A   M   J   J   A   S   O   N

Host: Beech, maple, and oak
Identification: Note the hollow spots.

144

0 – *Plagodis serinaria*
Lemon Plagodis Moth

6841 - *Plagodis kuetzingi*
Purple Plagodis Moth

6842 – *Plagodis phlogosaria*
Straight-lined Plagodis Moth

6843 – *Plagodis fervidaria*
Fervid Plagodis Moth

6844 – *Plagodis alcoolaria*
Hollow-spotted Plagodis Moth

6863 - *Caripeta divisata*
Gray Spruce Looper Moth

| M | A | M | J | J | A | S | O | N |

Host: Spruce

Identification: The design on the wings resembles a mask from a masquerade ball.

6869 - *Caripeta aretaria*
Southern Pine Moth

| M | A | M | J | J | A | S | O | N |

Host: Pine

Identification: This moth is rare in Ohio with only a few sightings. Look for the rust-colored mask on the brown frosted background.

6885 - *Besma quercivoraria*
Oak Besma Moth

| M | A | M | J | J | A | S | O | N |

Host: Oak, elm, poplar, and willow

Identification: The jagged hindwing margin resemble a euchlaena, but this species has very prominent dark veins on the wings.

6894 - *Lambdina fervidaria*
Curve-lined Looper Moth

| M | A | M | J | J | A | S | O | N |

Host: Oak, ash, and hemlock

Identification: The brown speckling on the beige background, in combination with the brown mask, is distinctive. The yellow-headed looper is very similar and may not be distinguishable from the curve-lined.

146

6863 - *Caripeta divisata*
Gray Spruce Looper Moth

6869 - *Caripeta aretaria*
Southern Pine Looper Moth

6885 – *Besma quercivoraria*
Oak Besma Moth

6894 - *Lambdina fervidaria*
Curve-lined Looper Moth

6941 - *Eusarca confusaria*
Confused Eusarca Moth

| M | A | M | J | J | A | S | O | N |

Host: Sunflower Family

Identification: The dark line in the middle of the forewing makes an abrupt turn away from the apex of the wing, In addition, this moth sports four small, dark spots, one on each wing.

6963 - *Tetracis crocallata*
Yellow Slant-line Moth

| M | A | M | J | J | A | S | O | N |

Host: Alder, sumac, and willow

Identification: The dark line on the forewing extends all the way to the apex. Also note the small spot on each forewing.

6964 - *Tetracis cachexiata*
White Slant-line Moth

| M | A | M | J | J | A | S | O | N |

Host: Most deciduous and coniferous trees

Identification: This moth is a pale version of the yellow slant-line. This species also lacks the small spot on each forewing.

6966 - *Eutrapela clemataria*
Curve-toothed Geometer

| M | A | M | J | J | A | S | O | N |

Host: Many tree species

Identification: Curve-toothed geometer has a hooked wing tip much like arched hooktip (Hodge's #6251). Curve-toothed has a much more jagged hindwing margin.

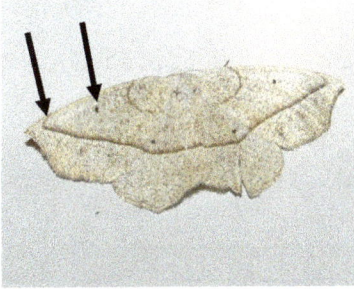

6941 - *Eusarca confusaria*
Confused Eusarca

6963 - *Tetracis crocallata*
Yellow Slant-line Moth

6964 – *Tetracis cachexiata*
White Slant-Line Moth

6966 – *Eutrapela clemataria*
Curve-toothed Geometer

6982 - *Prochoerodes transversata*
Large Maple Spanworm Moth

| | | | | | | | |
|M|A|M|J|J|A|S|O|N|

Host: Maple and several other deciduous trees

Identification: The wingtip does not have as long of a tooth as the previous species. The hindwing, jagged, "wood-burned" markings can be quite subtle to very bold and obvious. Likewise with the "wood-burned" markings closer to the head on the forewings.

6987 - *Antepione thisoaria*
Variable Antepione Moth

| | | | | | | | |
|M|A|M|J|J|A|S|O|N|

Host: Maple, apple, persimmon, and sumac

Identification: The moth has multiple forms, some of which are quite beautiful. The form pictured on the opposite page somewhat resembles the crocus geometers. The 'wood burning' marks near forewing apex are consistent across most forms.

6982 - *Prochoerodes transversata*
Large Maple Spanworm Moth

6987 - *Antepione thisoaria*
Variable Antepione Moth

Emerald Moths

This is the general common name given to the group of small, green Inch-worm Moths. At Butterfly Ridge, Emeralds are typically found more so in the early summer months and are always a crowd favorite!

....

7046 - *Nemoria bistriaria*
Red-fringed Emerald Moth

M	A	M	J	J	A	S	O	N

Host: White oak
Identification: Look for two white lines on each wing and the red/tan fringe on the wing margins.

....

7048 - *Nemoria mimosaria*
White-fringed Emerald Moth

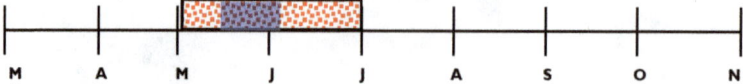

M	A	M	J	J	A	S	O	N

Host: Primarily oak, but uses several other tree species as well.
Identification: Look for two white lines on each wing but with a white fringe, unlike the previous species. This species also lacks the spot in the cell of each wing.

....

7053 - *Dichorda iridaria*
Showy Emerald Moth

M	A	M	J	J	A	S	O	N

Host: Sumac and poison ivy
Identification: Notice that the forewings have two white lines while the hindwings have but one. This moth also has a white frosting throughout. Rare at Butterfly Ridge despite an abundance of both sumac and poison ivy.

7046 – *Nemoria bistriaria*
**Red-fringed Emerald
Moth**

7048 - *Nemoria mimosaria*
**White-fringed Emerald
Moth**

7053 - *Dichorda iridaria*
Showy Emerald

7058 - *Synchlora aerata*
Wavy-lined Emerald Moth

M	A	M	J	J	A	S	O	N

Host: Plants in the Sunflower Family

Identification: This species is much like the white-fringed except for the very obvious white veins in the wings. The white veins make this species quite showy.

7071 - *Chlorochlamys chloroleucaria*
Blackberry Looper Moth

M	A	M	J	J	A	S	O	N

Host: Blackberry, dogbane, goldenrod

Identification: This species is much like the red-fringed except that the fringe is white/cream color. Also note that the inner white line on the forewing makes an abrupt turn as it nears the wing   margin. This species is thought to have at least two generations   during the season. Our data would suggest three generations.

7058 - *Synchlora aerata*
Wavy-lined Emerald Moth

7071 – *Chlorochlamys chloroleucaria*
Blackberry Looper Moth

7105 - *Idaea scintillularia*
Diminutive Wave Moth

M	A	M	J	J	A	S	O	N

Host: Unknown

Identification: This species is unlike any of our other moths. It is very small with a wingspan about a centimeter and wings have a sparkly, plastic appearance. Highly unusual!

....

7132 - *Pleuroprucha insulsaria*
Common Tan Wave Moth

M	A	M	J	J	A	S	O	N

Host: A wide variety of woody and herbaceous plants

Identification: This species is the same general size and shape as the emerald moths. Look for the tan base color with very subtle parallel wavy lines in the wings.

....

7136 - *Cyclophora packardi*
Packard's Wave Moth

M	A	M	J	J	A	S	O	N

Host: A wide variety of woody and herbaceous plants

Identification: This moth is similar to common tan wave but notice that some of the 'waves' are a series of unconnected black dots and that there is also a hollow spot on each wing.

7105 - *Idaea scintillularia*
Diminutive Wave Moth

7132 - *Pleuroprucha insulsaria*
Common Tan Wave Moth

7136 - *Cyclophora packardi*
Packard's Wave Moth

7146 - *Haematopis grataria*
Chickweed Geometer

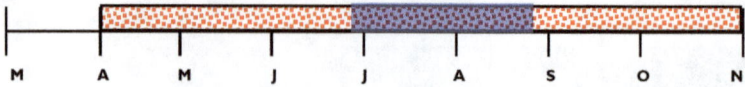

M A M J J A S O N

Host: Chickweed and clover

Identification: The pink lines and edging is unique among our Ohio moths. This species is frequently found in the daytime in lawns.

7159 - *Scopula limboundata*
Large Lace-border Moth

M A M J J A S O N

Host: Cherry, apple, clover, blueberry, and dandelion

Identification: The lace-border moth resembles an angle moth but lacks the apical notch and large black spots in the forewings. Instead, this moth has dingy gray spots near the margins of all wings.

7181 - *Lophosis labeculata*
Stained Lophosis Moth

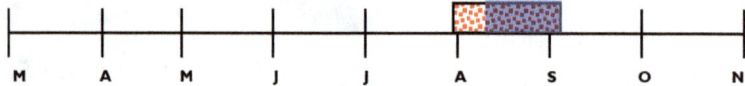

M A M J J A S O N

Host: Unknown

Identification: Very similar to mint-loving pyrausta (#5071) but larger and lacking noticeable snout.

7196 - *Eulithis diversilineata*
Lesser Grapevine Looper Moth

M A M J J A S O N

Host: Virginia creeper and grape

Identification: Note the multiple, alternating bands with a tooth that extends into a frosted area nearly to the wing edge.

7146 - *Haematopis grataria*
Chickweed Geometer

7159 – *Scopula limboundata*
Large Lace-border Moth

7181 – *Lophosis labeculata*
Stained Lophosis Moth

7196 – *Eulithis diversilineata*
Lesser Grapevine Looper Moth

7214 - *Gandaritis atricolorata*
Dark-banded Geometer Moth

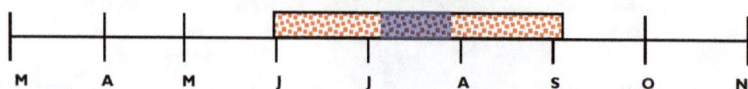

M   A   M   J   J   A   S   O   N

Host: Unknown

Identification: Very little is known about this moth but the identification is simple. The dark base color with the boldly contrasting silver-yellow lines is unlike anything else.

7290 - *Coryphista meadii*
Barberry Geometer

M   A   M   J   J   A   S   O   N

Host: Barberry

Identification: The pink lines and edging is unique among our Ohio moths. This species is frequently found in the daytime in lawns.

7292 - *Rheumaptera prunivorata*
Ferguson's Scallop Shell Moth

M   A   M   J   J   A   S   O   N

Host: Unknown

Identification: Perhaps the easiest of our moths to identify due to the numerous, tightly packed, parallel lines.

7368 - *Xanthorhoe labradorensis*
Labrador Carpet Moth

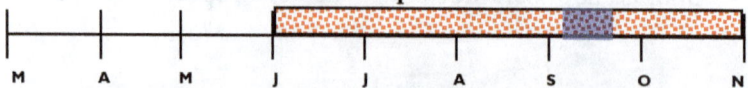

M   A   M   J   J   A   S   O   N

Host: A wide variety of woody and herbaceous plants.

Identification: Note the brown band in the middle of the wings.

7214 - *Gandaritis atricolorata*
Dark-banded Geometer

7290 - *Coryphista meadii*
Barberry Geometer

7292 – *Rheumaptera prunivorata*
Ferguson's Scallop Shell Moth

7368 - *Xanthorhoe labradorensis*
Labrador Carpet Moth

7388 - *Xanthorhoe ferrugata*
Red Twin-spot Moth

| | | | | | | | | |
|M|A|M|J|J|A|S|O|N|

Host: Chickweed, smartweed, and ground-ivy

Identification: The key identification feature of this moth is the pair of dark spots along the margin of the forewing.

7390 - *Xanthorhoe lacustrata*
Toothed Brown Carpet Moth

| | | | | | | | | |
|M|A|M|J|J|A|S|O|N|

Host: Birch, blackberry, hawthorn, and willow

Identification: This species is very similar to the red twin-spot, just lacking the two spots on the forewing, although there may be a vague discoloration in that same location of the wing.

7414 - *Orthonama obstipata*
Gem Moth

| | | | | | | | | |
|M|A|M|J|J|A|S|O|N|

Host: A variety of herbaceous plants.

Identification: This species is sexually dimorphic. The female is reddish with a prominent white circle, while the male is yellow-brown with a dark spot in place of the female's white circle. Both sexes are pictured on opposite page.

7416 - *Costaconvexa centrostrigaria*
Bent-line Carpet Moth

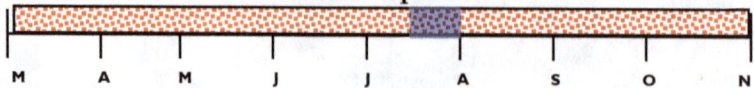

| | | | | | | | | |
|M|A|M|J|J|A|S|O|N|

Host: Smartweed

Identification: Similar in appearance to most carpet moths. Look for the dark spot on the forewing.

7388 - *Xanthorhoe ferrugata*
Red Twin-spot Moth

7390 - *Xanthorhoe lacustrata*
Toothed Brown Carpet

Female

Male

7414 - *Orthonama obstipata*
Gem Moth

7416 - *Costaconvexa centrostrigaria*
Bent-line Carpet Moth

7422 - *Hydrelia inornata*
Unadorned Carpet Moth

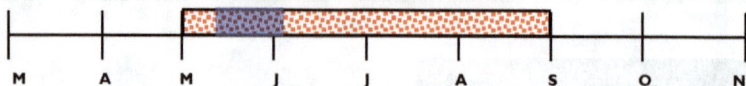

| M | A | M | J | J | A | S | O | N |

Host: Unknown

Identification: This moth is certainly a dressed down version of the other carpet moths in our area. The checked wing margins appear to be somewhat different from the others. Very little is known about this moth.

7440 - *Eubaphe mendica*
Beggar Moth

| M | A | M | J | J | A | S | O | N |

Host: Maple and violets

Identification: This pastel yellow moth with faded purple spots is unlike anything else at Butterfly Ridge.

7449 - *Eupithecia palpata*
Small Pine Looper Moth

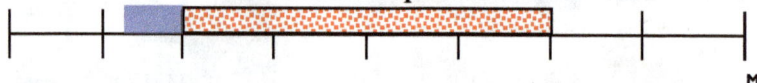

M

Host: Pine and hemlock

Identification: This moth is the classic pug moth size and shape but the brown color of both the body and wings is very unique.

7474 - *Eupithecia miserulata*
Common Eupithecia Moth

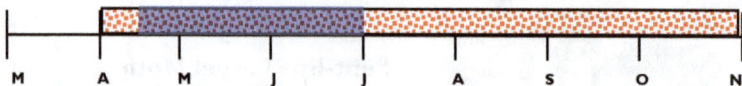

| M | A | M | J | J | A | S | O | N |

Host: A wide variety of woody and herbaceous plants

Identification: This moth is the classic pug moth size and shape and fairly unremarkable in appearance except for the prominent discal dots on the forewing.

7422 - *Hydrelia inornata*
Unadorned Carpet Moth

7440 - *Eubaphe mendica*
Beggar Moth

7449 - *Eupithecia palpata*
Small Pine Looper Moth

7474 - *Eupithecia miserulata*
Common Eupithecia Moth

7586.1 - *Eupithecia absinthiata*

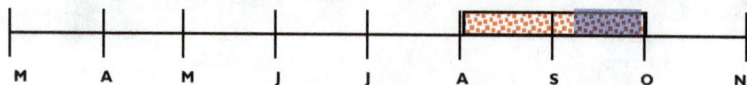

M	A	M	J	J	A	S	O	N

Host: Unknown

Identification: The constricted black band on the abdomen seems to set this moth apart from the other *Eupithecia* species in our area. Otherwise, this moth is very similar in appearance to common eupithecia.

7625 - *Pasiphila rectangulata*
Green Pug Moth

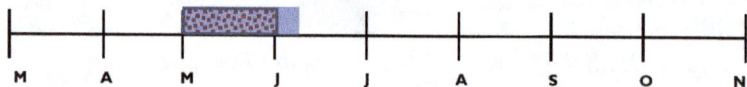

M	A	M	J	J	A	S	O	N

Host: Apple, cherry, pear, and hawthorn

Identification: The only pug moth in our area that is green. This moth is rarely observed in southeast Ohio.

7639 - *Cladara atroliturata*
Scribbler Moth

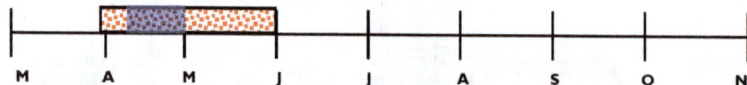

M	A	M	J	J	A	S	O	N

Host: Apple, birch, maple, and willow

Identification: The alternating squiggly green, white, and black bands is very unlike any other moth in our area. The closest look -a-like would be the green sallow moths in the Noctuid group.

7647 - *Heterophleps triguttaria*
Three-spotted Fillip Moth

M	A	M	J	J	A	S	O	N

Host: Maple

Identification: The only identification marks on this drab moth are the three prominent dark spots on the forewing margin.

7586.1 - *Eupithecia absinthiata*

7625 - *Pasiphila rectangulata*
Green Pug Moth

7639 - *Cladara atroliturata*
Scribbler Moth

7647 - *Heterophleps triguttaria*
Three-spotted Fillip Moth

7648 - *Dyspteris abortivaria*
Badwing Moth

| M | A | M | J | J | A | S | O | N |

Host: Grape and Virginia creeper

Identification: This moth looks like it should be in the emerald group but it is not. The hindwings are MUCH smaller than the forewings, which makes it very different from the emeralds.

Mimallonidae - Sack-bearer Moths

The caterpillars of this group build little portable cases out of silk, frass, and leaves, thus traveling with their nest.

7659 - *Lacosoma chiridota*
Scalloped Sack-bearer Moth

| M | A | M | J | J | A | S | O | N |

Host: Oak

Identification: These moths have deeply scalloped wings and hooked wing tips. They are also sexually dimorphic with males having dark forewings while females have red-gold forewings. Pictured is a female. This species overwinters inside of its 'sack' as a caterpillar.

7648 - *Dyspteris abortivaria*
Badwing Moth

7659 - *Lacosoma chiridota*
Scalloped Sack-bearer Moth

Bombycidae - Silk-worm Moths

While most lepidopteran caterpillars have the ability to spin silk, the larvae of this family spins silk that is strong enough to use for fabric.

··

7663 - *Apatelodes torrefacta*
Spotted Apatelodes Moth

M	A	M	J	J	A	S	O	N

Host: Cherry, ash, maple, and oak

Identification: This is one of our most recognizable moths, with the hindwings held beneath the forewings, exposing the complete abdomen. It also has prominent dark spots on the inner part of the forewing.

··

7665 - *Olcedostera angelica*
Angel Moth

M	A	M	J	J	A	S	O	N

Host: Ash and lilac

Identification: Note the large silver spots near the apical notch of the forewings.

7663 – *Apatelodes torrefacta*
Spotted Apatelodes Moth

7665 – *Olceclostera* **angelica**
Angel Moth

Lasiocampidae - Tent Caterpillar Moths

Females of this group lay eggs in large masses encased in a material that hardens when exposed to air. The caterpillars then spin large silken nests on the tree branch that will house all of the caterpillars in the brood.

7670 - *Tolype velleda*
Large Tolype Moth

M	A	M	J	J	A	S	O	N

Host: Several deciduous tree and shrub species

Identification: This late season moth is easily recognized by the dingy gray wings contrasting with the white, furry head and thorax. Also note that the abdomen sticks out below the wings.

7683 - *Artace cribrarius*
Dot-lined White Moth

M	A	M	J	J	A	S	O	N

Host: Oak, cherry, and rose

Identification: This moth is easily recognized by the black dots on white wings that form a linear arrangement. Also note the golden colored antennae on the white head. This moth has two distinct seasons; mid-summer and again in mid-autumn.

7687 - *Phyllodesma americana*
Lappet Moth

M	A	M	J	J	A	S	O	N

Host: Oak, cherry, and rose

Identification: While the colors vary on this moth, the light bands with dark borders are fairly consistent. Quite unusual is the scalloping on the trailing edge of the forewing.

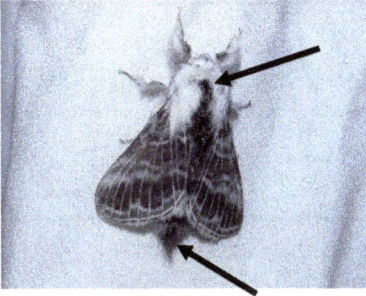

7670 – *Tolype velleda*
Large Tolype Moth

7683 – *Artace cribrarius*
Dot-lined White Moth

7687 – *Phyllodesma americana*
Lappet Moth

7698 - *Malacosoma disstria*
Forest Tent Caterpillar Moth

| M | A | M | J | J | A | S | O | N |

Host: Several deciduous tree species including cherry and oak
Identification: Note the parallel dark curved lines on the fore-wing. The larva nest together in large numbers and can defoliate large sections of the tree canopy.

Saturniidae - Giant Silkworm Moths

These are the very large moths that usually grab people's attention. Most do not have functioning mouth parts. Males generally have broader, larger antennae which are more effective in detecting pheromones released by the females. Wingspan is frequently more than two inches.

7704 - *Eacles imperialis*
Imperial Moth

| M | A | M | J | J | A | S | O | N |

Host: Several deciduous tree and shrub species
Identification: The Imperial Moth's markings can vary. Males are normally more heavily marked than females. Generally look for red blotching on a yellow background.

7706 - *Citheronia regalis*
Regal Moth

| M | A | M | J | J | A | S | O | N |

Host: Several deciduous tree species
Identification: This moth has a very unique appearance with a gray/brown base color, red wing veins, and yellow speckles. This moth also goes by the name Royal Walnut Moth. The caterpillar is known as a Hickory Horned Devil because of its fearsome appearance.

7698 - *Malacosoma disstria*

Forest Tent Caterpillar Moth

Giant Silkworm and Royal Moths

7704 – *Eacles imperialis*

Imperial Moth

7706 – *Citheronia regalis*

Regal Moth

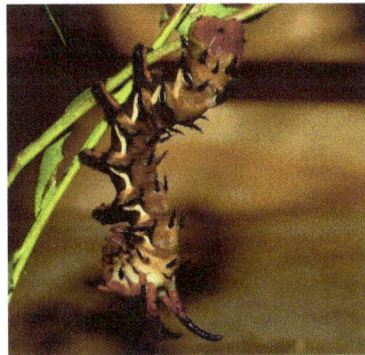

7708 - *Citheronia sepulcralis*
Pine Devil Moth

M	A	M	J	J	A	S	O	N

Host: Pine

Identification: Of our big moths, this is the only one that is a solid gray/tan color. Also note the gold spots near where the forewing attaches to the body.

7715 - *Dryocampa rubicunda*
Rosy Maple Moth

M	A	M	J	J	A	S	O	N

Host: Maple, beech, oak, and sycamore

Identification: The combination of pink and yellow is unlike anything else that flies at Butterfly Ridge. The Rosy Maple Moth is the most frequently encountered member of the Saturnid family at Butterfly Ridge.

7708 – *Citheronia sepulcralis*
Pine Devil Moth

7715 – *Dryocampa rubicunda*
Rosy Maple Moth

7716 - *Anisota stigma*
Spiny Oakworm Moth

M   A   M   J   J   A   S   O   N

Host: Oak

Identification: Of our big moths, this is the only one that has a solid orange base color. Note the silver spots on the forewings. This species also has dark speckles on the wings.

7723 - *Anisota virginiensis*
Pink-striped Oakworm Moth

M   A   M   J   J   A   S   O   N

Host: Oak

Identification: This species is much like the Spiny Oakworm except that this moth lacks the dark speckles on the orange wings.

7730 - *Hemileuca maia*
Buck Moth

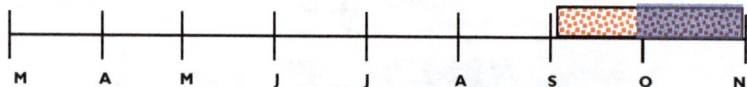

M   A   M   J   J   A   S   O   N

Host: Oak

Identification: This moth has black wings with broad white bands on each wing. In addition there is bright orange on the body. The Buck Moth generally does NOT come to the lights. This is a day flyer and can be seen frequently flying through autumn woodlots. This is one of our latest of the big moths.

7716 – *Anisota stigma*
Spiny Oakworm Moth

7723 - *Anisota virginiensis*
Pink-striped Oakworm Moth

7730 – *Hemileuca maia*
Buck Moth

7746 - *Automeris io*
Io Moth

M   A   M   J   J   A   S   O   N

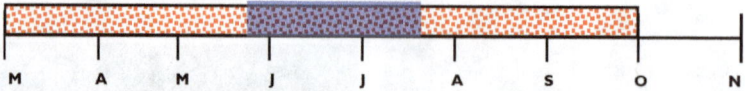

Host: A wide variety of plants

Identification: This moth is easily recognized by the large eyespots and red blush on the hindwings. The forewings of the Io Moth slightly resemble those of the Imperial Moth, but the Io is typically smaller. The Io is sexually dimorphic with the male being yellow and the female more of a reddish-tan color. The spines on the caterpillar yield a painful sting to the person who touches them.

7757 - *Antheraea polyphemus*
Polyphemus Moth

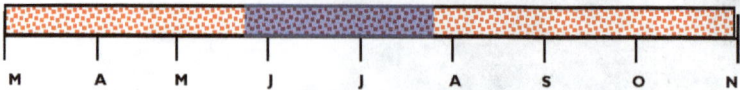

M   A   M   J   J   A   S   O   N

Host: Oak, birch, maple, hickory, and grape

Identification: The Polyphemus is easily recognized by the pink brackets on the inner part of the forewing as well as the single eyespot on each wing. It also has a single eyespot on each hindwing, however these spots are normally concealed by the forewings.

7746 – *Automeris io*
Io Moth

7757 – *Antheraea polyphemus*
Polyphemus Moth

7758 - *Actias luna*
Luna Moth

| M | A | M | J | J | A | S | O | N |

Host: Hickory, Walnut, Sumac, and other tree species

Identification: With its green color and long tails, the Luna Moth is probably the most recognized moth in the United States. This species is relatively common at Butterfly Ridge.

7764 - *Callosamia promethea*
Promethea Moth

| M | A | M | J | J | A | S | O | N |

Host: Many deciduous tree species

Identification: Pictured is a female, as evidenced by the red color, huge abdomen, and narrow antennae. Male Promethea are very dark, nearly black in color. It is very difficult to tell the Promethea Moth from the next species, the Tulip Tree Moth. One helpful feature is that male Prometheas generally do not come to lights, whereas male Tulip Tree Moths will. The white markings on the Tulip Tree Moth tend to be much bolder and prominent than on the Promethea. At Butterfly Ridge, the Tulip Tree Moth is much more common than the Promethea Moth.

7758 - *Actias luna*
Luna Moth

7764 – *Callosamia promethea*
Promethea Moth

7765 - Callosamia angulifera
Tulip Tree Moth

M	A	M	J	J	A	S	O	N

Host: Tulip Tree

Identification: Pictured is a male, as evidenced by the dark brown wings. Female Tulip Tree Moths are yellow to orange-brown in color. It is very difficult to tell the Tulip Tree Moth from the previous species, the Promethea Moth. One helpful feature is that male Prometheas generally do not come to lights, whereas male Tulip Tree Moths will. The white markings on the Tulip Tree Moth tend to be much bolder and prominent than on the Promethea.

....

7767 - Hyalophora cecropia
Cecropia Moth

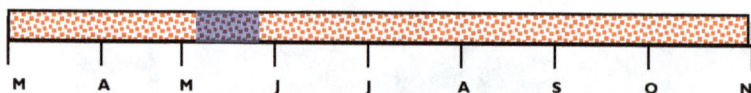

M	A	M	J	J	A	S	O	N

Host: Many deciduous tree species

Identification: The Cecropia is easily distinguished from the Promethea and Tulip Tree Moths by the broad red band and large white spot on the hindwings viewable from both sides of the wings. At Butterfly Ridge, the moth pictured to the right is the only Cecropia that has been observed in several years. This may be in part because the Cecropia doesn't tend to fly until very early morning. However, throughout the Midwest, Cecropia numbers are said to be in decline, largely due to habitat loss from urbanization and agriculture.

7765 – *Callosamia angulifera*
Tulip-tree Silkmoth

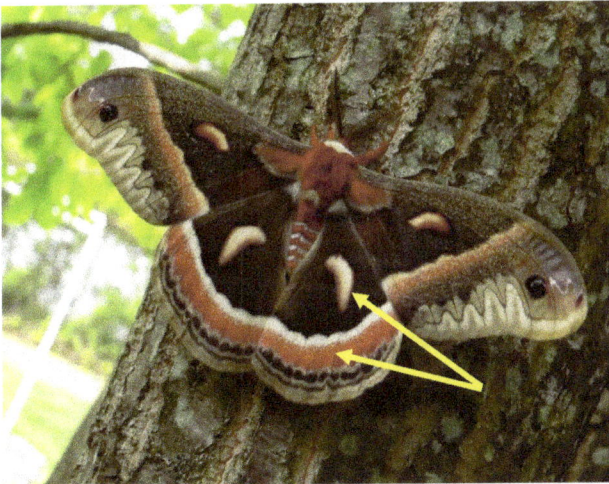

7767 – *Hyalophora cecropia*
Cecropia Moth

Sphingidae - Sphinx Moths

These are large moths some of which fly during the day, nectaring on flowers. Unlike the Giant Silkmoths, the Sphinx Moths do have functioning mouth parts. The Sphinx Moths readily divide themselves into two groups, rounded forewing tips and squared-off forewings. The hindwings are frequently hidden from view, especially in the round-tipped group.

7775 - *Manduca sexta*
Carolina Sphinx Moth

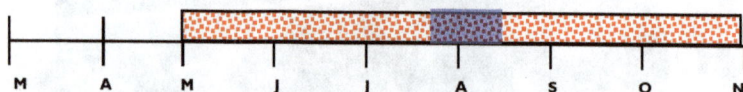

| M | A | M | J | J | A | S | O | N |

Host: Jimsonweed, tomato, pepper, and tobacco

Identification: There are several drab, gray sphinx moths. Carolina Sphinx is distinguished by the yellow spots on the sides of the abdomen. Considered to be a garden pest despite being native to the area.

7783 - *Manduca jasminearum*
Ash Sphinx Moth

| M | A | M | J | J | A | S | O | N |

Host: Ash and lilac

Identification: The Ash Sphinx can be recognized by the dark line that runs from the leading edge of the forewing to the trailing edge. Also look for the dark "collar" on this moth.

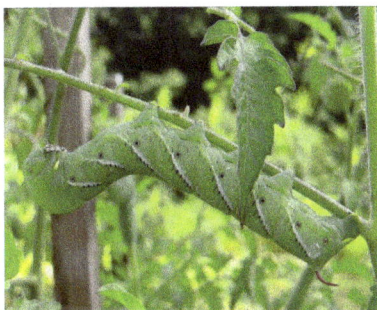

7775 - *Manduca sexta*
Carolina Sphinx Moth

7783 – *Manduca jasminearum*
Ash Sphinx Moth

7786 - *Ceratomia amyntor*
Elm Sphinx Moth

M	A	M	J	J	A	S	O	N

Host: Elm, cherry, and birch

Identification: Many of the round-tipped sphinx moths tend toward various shades of gray, the Elm Sphinx is definitely brown. Note the small white spots on the forewing as well as the darker shading on the sides of the head and in the middle of the forewing.

7787 - *Ceratomia undulosa*
Waved Sphinx Moth

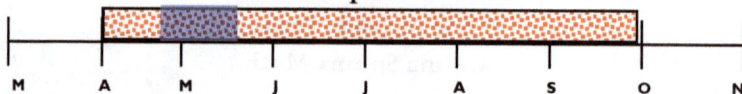

M	A	M	J	J	A	S	O	N

Host: Ash, oak, lilac and others

Identification: This species is much like other gray sphinx moths. The 'daggers' on the forewing help distinguish this moth from the others. The toothed line through the forewing is also distinctive.

7789 - *Ceratomia catalpae*
Catalpa Sphinx Moth

M	A	M	J	J	A	S	O	N

Host: Catalpa

Identification: There is a lot of variability in the appearance of the Catalpa Sphinx. Generally speaking the base color is a brown -gray. Where the antennae lay against the side of the head and thorax gives the appearance of white horns. There is a very distinct reniform spot on the forewings along with 3-4 obvious dark lines. Unfortunately, these individual characteristics are not unique among the round-tipped sphinxes. The caterpillars is quite colorful and notorious for braconid wasp infections.

7786 – *Ceratomia amyntor*
Elm Sphinx Moth

7787 - *Ceratomia undulosa*
Waved Sphinx Moth

7789 - *Ceratomia catalpa*
Catalpa Sphinx

7809 - *Sphinx kalmiae*
Laurel Sphinx Moth

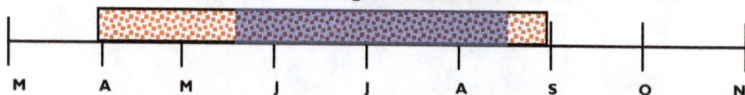

M A M J J A S O N

Host: Ash, lilac, and privet

Identification: One of the easiest to identify sphinx moths because of the wood grain appearance of the forewings. The name is very misleading. This moth is actually named after early botanist Peter Kalm, NOT after the scientific name of Mountain Laurel, a common shrub in the Hocking Hills of Ohio.

7816 - *Lapara coniferarum*
Southern Pine Sphinx Moth

M A M J J A S O N

Host: Pine

Identification: Several diagnostic features make this moth easy to identify. First is the pink-rust color on the inside edge of the forewings. Secondly is the very prominent two dark lines on each forewing. Finally is the "dripping icicle" look of the post-medial line on the forewings.

7809 – *Sphinx kalmiae*
Laurel Sphinx Moth

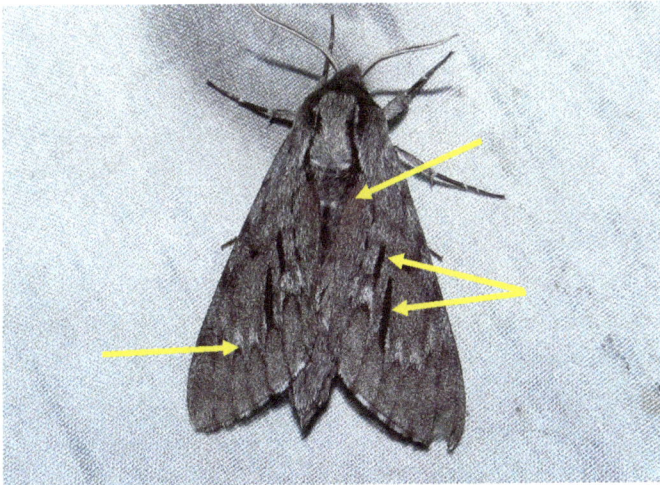

7816 – *Lapara coniferarum*
Southern Pine Sphinx Moth

7824 - *Paonias exaecata*
Blind-eyed Sphinx Moth

M   A   M   J   J   A   S   O   N

Host: Several deciduous trees and shrubs

Identification: Notice how the hindwings are exposed above the forewings, rather than below. Also notice the dark "violin" on top of the body. Blind-eyed Sphinx is the first of the sphinx moths with the "squared-off" forewings as opposed to the rounded forewings.

7825 - *Paonias myops*
Small-eyed Sphinx Moth

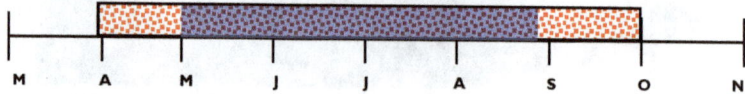

M   A   M   J   J   A   S   O   N

Host: Birch, poplar, cherry, and willow

Identification: Notice the dark stripes on the back of the head and thorax rather than the violin design. In addition, Small-eyed Sphinx has much more yellow in the wings.

7826 - *Paonias astylus*
Huckleberry Sphinx Moth

M   A   M   J   J   A   S   O   N

Host: Blueberry, huckleberry, and cherry

Identification: This beautiful sphinx moth is relatively rare in Ohio, and Butterfly Ridge was blessed to document several in 2017. Similar to Small-eyed Sphinx, Huckleberry is more pink and lacks the second indentation on the margin of the forewing.

7824 – *Paonias excaecata*
Blind-eyed Sphinx Moth

7825 – *Paonias myops*
Small-eyed Sphinx Moth

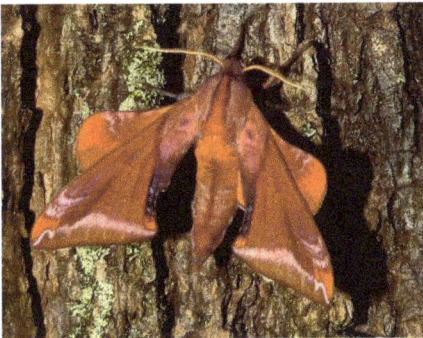

7826 – *Paonias astylus*
Huckleberry Sphinx Moth

7827 - *Amorpha juglandis*
Walnut Sphinx Moth

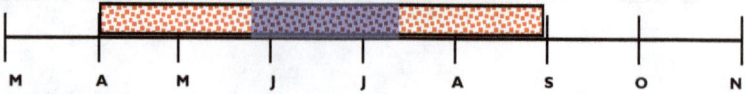

| M | A | M | J | J | A | S | O | N |

Host: Walnut, hickory, and cherry

Identification: The Walnut Sphinx is one of the more drably marked of the squared-tip group of sphinxes. It has varying degrees of shading on a tan to nearly pink base color.

7828 - *Pachysphinx modesta*
Big Poplar Sphinx Moth

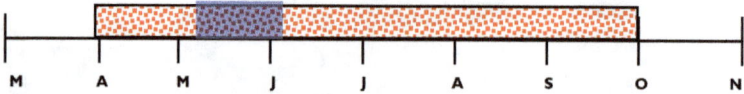

| M | A | M | J | J | A | S | O | N |

Host: Cottonwood and willow

Identification: Similar to the Walnut Sphinx but with bolder, but more limited banding. In addition, the hindwing, if the moth offers you a glimpse, is quite stunning with red, blue, and black.

7859 - *Eumorpha pandorus*
Pandorus Sphinx Moth

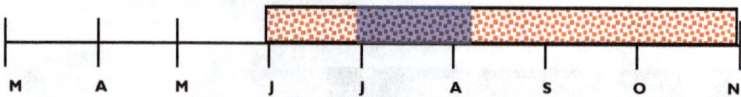

| M | A | M | J | J | A | S | O | N |

Host: Grape and Virginia creeper

Identification: The green mottled color of Pandorus Sphinx is not only beautiful but also unique. The only other moth with a similar pattern is the Virginia Creeper Sphinx which is sort of a miniature version of Pandorus.

7827 – *Amorpha juglandis*
Walnut Sphinx Moth

7828 – *Pachysphinx modesta*
Big Poplar Sphinx Moth

7859 – *Eumorpha pandorus*
Pandorus Sphinx Moth

The Hummingbird Moths

The term 'Hummingbird Moth' typically refers to Sphinx Moths which fly during the day and hover over flowers as they imbibe nectar, thus appearing at a distance to be a hummingbird. Many of these 'Hummingbird Moths' have transparent wings, a character that matches two of the three in our area.

7853 - *Hemaris thysbe*
Hummingbird Clearwing Moth

| M | A | M | J | J | A | S | O | N |

Host: Honeysuckle, viburnum, and snowberry

Identification: This moth is recognized by the maroon and olive-tan color. These moths love to nectar on Bergamot (*Monarda fistulosa*).

7855 - *Hemaris diffinis*
Snowberry Clearwing Moth

| M | A | M | J | J | A | S | O | N |

Host: Honeysuckle and snowberry

Identification: This moth is much like the previous species, but with a black-yellow color pattern, very much resembling a bumble bee! These moths love to nectar on Bergamot (*Monarda fistulosa*).

7873 - *Amphion floridensis*
Nessus Sphinx Moth

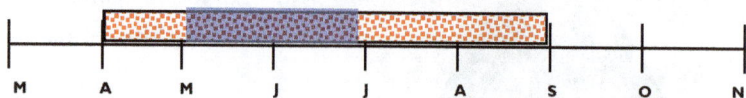

| M | A | M | J | J | A | S | O | N |

Host: Grape

Identification: Nessus Sphinx is a bee mimic, with brightly colored stripes on a dark body. This moth hovers above the flowers from which it is drinking nectar, much like a hummingbird. Not likely to see this one during the night but rather in the daytime.

7853 - *Hemaris thysbe*
**Hummingbird Clearwing
Moth**

7855 - *Hemaris diffinis*
Snowberry Clearwing Moth

7873 - *Amphion floridensis*
Nessus Sphinx Moth

7870 - *Sphecodina abbottii*
Abbott's Sphinx Moth

M	A	M	J	J	A	S	O	N

Host: Grape

Identification: A fresh Abbott's Sphinx has a beautiful wood grain look. But even worn individuals will have the bright yellow hindwing and the tuft of yellow hairs on the abdomen. A common moth at Butterfly Ridge in May and June.

7871 - *Deidamia inscriptum*
Lettered Sphinx Moth

M	A	M	J	J	A	S	O	N

Host: Grape and Virginia creeper

Identification: Two things make this moth an easy identification. First is the dark spot on the apical notch against a lighter background. Secondly is the very distinct line between dark and light just outside of the post-medial band. During its season, this is one of the most common moths at Butterfly Ridge.

7885 - *Darapsa myron*
Virginia Creeper Sphinx Moth

M	A	M	J	J	A	S	O	N

Host: Grape and Virginia creeper

Identification: An easy one to identify as this is one of only two green sphinx moths in our area, and the only one that has been found at Butterfly Ridge. The other green sphinx, Pandorus Sphinx, is much larger and has a mosaic of green and tan blocks on the wings rather than simple bands.

7870 – *Sphecodina abbottii*
Abbot's Sphinx Moth

7871 – *Deidamia inscriptum*
Lettered Sphinx Moth

7885 – *Darapsa myron*
Virginia Creeper Sphinx Moth

7886 - *Darapsa choerilus*
Azalea Sphinx Moth

| M | A | M | J | J | A | S | O | N |

Host: Azalea, Blueberry, and sour-gum
Identification: Similar to Virginia Creeper Sphinx except with a red base color rather than green. The forewing tips are slightly hooked.

7890 - *Xylophanes tersa*
Tersa Sphinx Moth

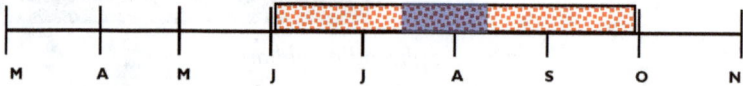

| M | A | M | J | J | A | S | O | N |

Host: Catalpa
Identification: This beautiful moth is a relatively rare find. The tight wood-grain look is very unique.

7894 - *Hyles lineata*
White-lined Sphinx Moth

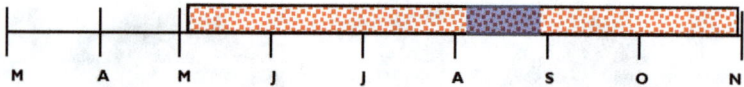

| M | A | M | J | J | A | S | O | N |

Host: A wide range of plants
Identification: This beautiful moth is sometimes referred to as a hummingbird moth due to its tendency to hover above flowers while it nectars. With no less than ten documented host plants, you would think they would be more common than they are. The wing pattern on this moth is so unique it will not be confused with anything else in North America.

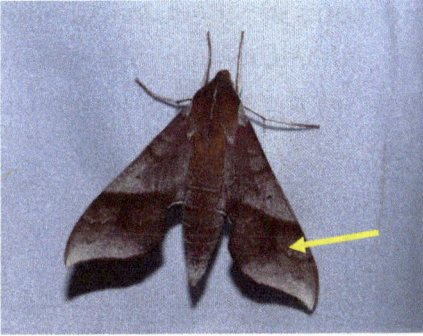

7886 – *Darapsa choerilus*
Azalea Sphinx Moth

7890 – *Xylophanthes tersa*
Tersa Sphinx Moth

7894 – *Hyles lineata*
**White-lined
Sphinx Moth**

Notodontidae - Prominent Moths

The Prominent Moths come in two forms. The first is what I refer to as "cigar moths" which have a rolled appearance. The first two moths in the section fall into this category. The other prominents look like typical moths. A common feature of the group is very furry legs.

7895 - *Clostera albosigma*
Sigmoid Prominent Moth

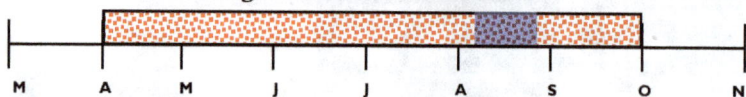

M	A	M	J	J	A	S	O	N

Host: Willow and poplar

Identification: The white 'S' on the side of this moth is a dead giveaway. The caterpillars of this species form large communal nests in their host tree.

7902 - 7914 - *Datana sp.*
Datana Moth

M	A	M	J	J	A	S	O	N

Host: Several deciduous tree species

Identification: There are several species that are nearly impossible to tell apart without caterpillars.

7915 - *Nadata gibbosa*
White-dotted Prominent Moth

M	A	M	J	J	A	S	O	N

Host: Oak and beech

Identification: Look for one or two very small white dots on the yellow forewing. This species also tends to have a yellow top-knot on its head (hard to see in this photo).

Prominent Moths

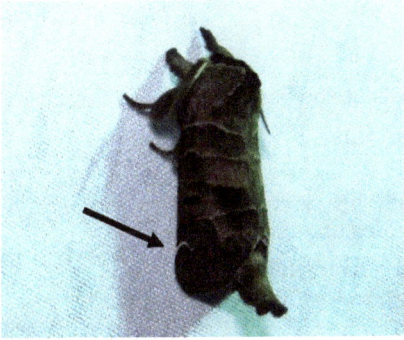

7895 – *Clostera albosigma*
Sigmoid Prominent Moth

7902-7914 – *Datana sp.*
Datana Moth

7915 – *Nadata gibbosa*
**White-dotted Prominent
Moth**

Oval-based Prominent Moth

M A M J J A S O N

Host: Maple
Identification: The brown ovals at the base of the forewings are unique among our prominent moths.

7920 - *Peridea angulosa*
Angulose Prominent Moth

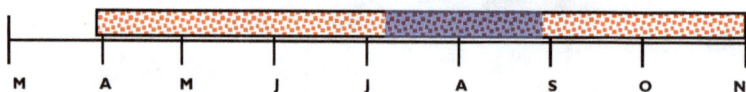

M A M J J A S O N

Host: Oak
Identification: Much like the Chocolate Prominent, but the mask on Angulose retains the same color as the rest of the wing.

7921 - *Peridea ferruginea*
Chocolate Prominent Moth

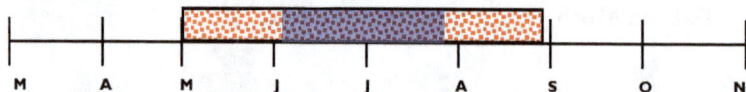

M A M J J A S O N

Host: Birch
Identification: The chocolate brown mask on the otherwise gray wings is a good identification tool for this moth. Usually there is also some brown near the head.

7922 - *Pheosia rimosa*
Black-rimmed Prominent Moth

M A M J J A S O N

Host: Poplar and willow
Identification: The combination of wing shape, wing color, and dark head almost makes this moth look like a giant fly! The light color in the wings bookended on each side with dark is quite unique, at least among the Prominents.

7919 – *Peridea basitriens*
**Oval-based
Prominent Moth**

7920 – *Peridea angulosa*
**Angulose
Prominent Moth**

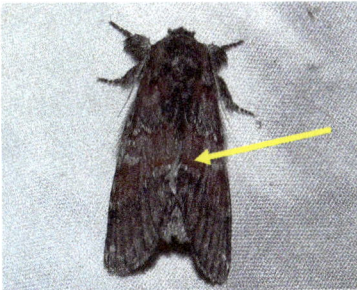

7921 – *Peridea ferruginea*
Chocolate Prominent Moth

7922 – *Pheosia rimosa*
Black-rimmed Prominent Moth

7924 - *Odontosia elegans*
Elegant Prominent Moth

| M | A | M | J | J | A | S | O | N |

Host: Poplar

Identification: The smooth chocolate brown with darker fine lines is very unique among our Butterfly Ridge moths. Also note that this moth has the classic top-knot like many of the Prominents.

7929 - *Nerice bidentata*
Double-toothed Prominent Moth

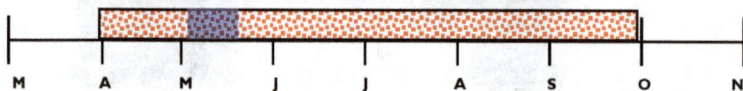

| M | A | M | J | J | A | S | O | N |

Host: Elm

Identification: This moth is aptly named based on the two prominent brown teeth on the light background.

7930 - *Ellida caniplaga*
Linden Prominent Moth

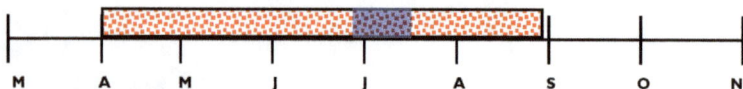

| M | A | M | J | J | A | S | O | N |

Host: Linden (Basswood)

Identification: This gray moth is poorly marked. Look for the three (sometimes four) prominent, short lines on the forewings. The caterpillar of this species is rarely seen since it feed high in the tree canopy.

7931 - *Gluphisia septentrionis*
Common Gluphisia Moth

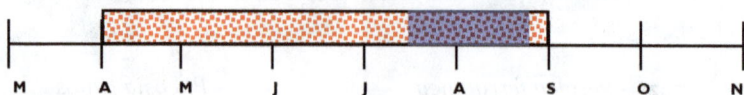

| M | A | M | J | J | A | S | O | N |

Host: Poplar

Identification: This moth is recognized by a brown 'mask' on the gray background of the forewings. Sometimes the mask is very subtle.

7924 - *Odontosia elegans*
Elegant Prominent Moth

7929 - *Nerice bidentata*
Double-toothed Prominent

7930 - *Ellida caniplaga*
Linden Prominent Moth

7931 - *Gluphisia septentrionis*
Common Gluphisia Moth

7936 - *Furcula borealis*
White Fercula Moth

M   A   M   J   J   A   S   O   N

Host: Cherry, willow, and poplar

Identification: This moth is easily identified by the dark mask on the white background.

7937 - *Furcula cinerea*
Gray Fercula Moth

M   A   M   J   J   A   S   O   N

Host: Birch, willow, and poplar

Identification: This moth is beautifully unique with its gray base color with yellow-orange spots.

7951-7955 - *Symmerista sp.*
Symmerista Moth

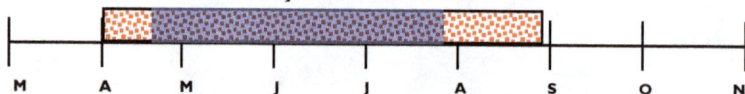

M   A   M   J   J   A   S   O   N

Host: Oak and other hardwoods

Identification: There are several species that are nearly impossible to tell apart without caterpillars. They all include a white patch on the leading edge of the forewing, with a more or less prominent tooth.

7957 - *Dasylophia anguina*
Black-spotted Prominent Moth

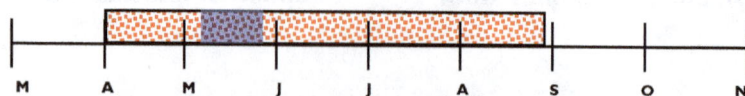

M   A   M   J   J   A   S   O   N

Host: Clover, Locust, and other Legumes.

Identification: There can be a lot of variability in the appearance of this moth. The black spots it is named after are marked by the yellow arrow.

7936 – *Furcula borealis*
White Furcula Moth

7937 – *Furcula cinereal*
Gray Furcula Moth

7951-7955 – *Symmerista sp.*
Symmerista Moth

7957 – *Dasylophia anguina*
Black-spotted Prominent Moth

7958- *Dasylophia thyatiroides*
Gray-patched Prominent Moth

| M | A | M | J | J | A | S | O | N |

Host: Legumes and hickory

Identification: Note the gray patch, which can vary widely in its level of contrast, on the forewing.

7974- *Misogada unicolor*
Drab Prominent Moth

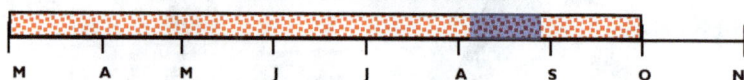

| M | A | M | J | J | A | S | O | N |

Host: Cottonwood and sycamore

Identification: The only thing prominent on this moth is the typical furry legs of this group. Otherwise this species is completely unmarked.

7983 - *Heterocampa obliqua*
Oblique Heterocampa Moth

| M | A | M | J | J | A | S | O | N |

Host: Oak

Identification: The key feature to look for is the rounded brown mark at the apical end of the forewing. Sometimes the rest of the forewing will have a greenish hue.

7990- *Heterocampa umbrata*
White-blotched Heterocampa Moth

| M | A | M | J | J | A | S | O | N |

Host: Oak

Identification: Note the rounded white patch at the apical end of the forewing. This white patch however sometimes appears simply lighter in color, not actually white.

7958 – *Dasylophia thyatiroides*
Gray-patched Prominent Moth

7974- *Misogada unicolor*
Drab Prominent Moth

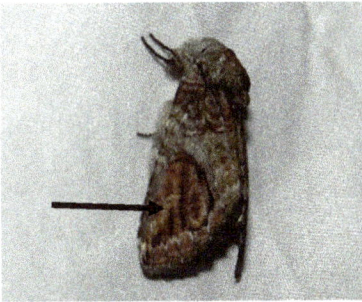

7983 – *Heterocampa obliqua*
Oblique Heterocampa Moth

7990- *Heterocampa umbrata*
White-blotched Heterocampa Moth

7999 - *Lochmaeus bilineata*
Double-lined Prominent Moth

M A M J J A S O N

Host: Beech, birch, elm, oak, and basswood

Identification: This moth is identified by the white lines which are outlined in black on each side. The lower most line also has prominent teeth on the margin.

8005 - *Schizura ipomaeae*
Morning-glory Prominent Moth

M A M J J A S O N

Host: Several deciduous trees and shrubs, but oddly not morning-glory

Identification: This is our darkest Prominent moth. Charcoal color with a straw-colored leading edge of the forewing.

8011 - *Schizura leptinoides*
Black-blotched Schizura Moth

M A M J J A S O N

Host: Several deciduous trees

Identification: The moth is identified using the dark blotch on the forewing (white arrow). At the head end of this blotch is a very distinct black spot (yellow arrow).

8012 - *Oligocentria semirufescens*
Red-washed Prominent Moth

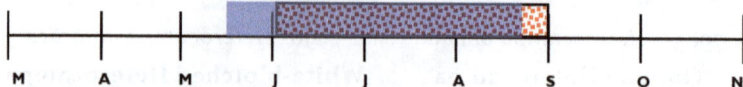

M A M J J A S O N

Host: Several deciduous trees and shrubs

Identification: This non-descript moth is a variety of colors, usually with varying degrees of red behind the head. The dark veins near the margins of the wings help a little in the identification.

7999 - *Lochmaeus bilineata*
**Double-lined Prominent
Moth**

8005 - *Schizura ipomaeae*
**Morning-glory Prominent
Moth**

8011 – *Schizura leptinoides*
**Black-blotched Schizura
Moth**

8012 – *Oligocentria
semirufescens*
**Red-washed Prominent
Moth**

Arctiidae - Tiger Moths

The Tiger Moths are normally quite colorful with forewings folding over each other. The caterpillars of Tiger Moths are usually quite furry and frequently referred to as Wooly Bears. One subgroup of the Tiger Moths is the Lichen Moths, whose caterpillars feed exclusively on lichen.

8046 - *Crambidia uniformis*
Uniform Lichen Moth

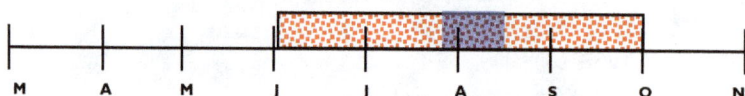

M	A	M	J	J	A	S	O	N

Host: Lichen

Identification: This very drab moth is beige-gray in color with the veins a slighter lighter shade of color.

8067 - *Cisthene plumbea*
Lead-colored Lichen Moth

M	A	M	J	J	A	S	O	N

Host: Lichen

Identification: The forewings of this species are a dingy gray framed by pastel yellow. The hindwings are salmon-colored. The Lead-colored Lichen Moth has two distinct broods, hence the break in the timeline above.

8072 - *Cisthene packardii*
Packard's Lichen Moth

M	A	M	J	J	A	S	O	N

Host: Lichen

Identification: Packard's is much like Lead-colored Lichen however with a more reddish blush rather than yellow. Packard's is also somewhat smaller.

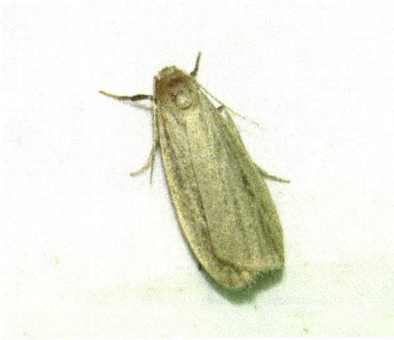

8046 - *Crambidia uniformis*
Uniform Lichen Moth

8067 – *Cisthene plumbea*
Lead-colored Lichen Moth

8072 – *Cisthene packardii*
Packard's Lichen Moth

8089 - *Hypoprepia miniata*
Scarlet-winged Lichen Moth

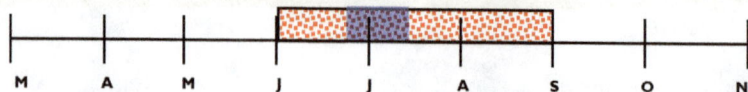

M A M J J A S O N

Host: Lichen

Identification: The bright red wings cannot be confused with anything else!

8090 - *Hypoprepia fucosa*
Painted Lichen Moth

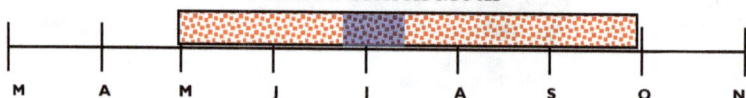

M A M J J A S O N

Host: Lichen

Identification: The blending of bright yellow and red is unique among our moths.

8098 - *Clemensia albata*
Little White Lichen Moth

M A M J J A S O N

Host: Lichen

Identification: The Little White Lichen Moth does not hardly resemble the other lichen moths in this book. In fact, this moth looks like a much smaller version of The Hebrew (#9285) with the black spots on the white background.

8107 - *Haploa clymene*
Clymene Moth

M A M J J A S O N

Host: Oak, willow, snakeroot, boneset, and Joe pye weed

Identification: When the forewings are held together, the dark pattern looks sort of like an angel. Hindwings are yellow. The Clymene Moth is frequently found during the day as well, usually among grasses and forbs.

8089 – *Hypoprepia miniata*
Scarlet-winged Lichen Moth

8090 – *Hypoprepia fucosa*
Painted Lichen Moth

8098 – *Clemensia albata*
Little White Lichen Moth

8107 - *Haploa clymene*
Clymene Moth

8111 - *Haploa lecontei*
Leconte's Haploa

| | | | | | | | | |
|M|A|M|J|J|A|S|O|N|

Host: Apple, blackberry, and peach

Identification: The forewings are a collection of white triangles framed in black.

8124 - *Virbia immaculata*
Immaculate Holomelina Moth

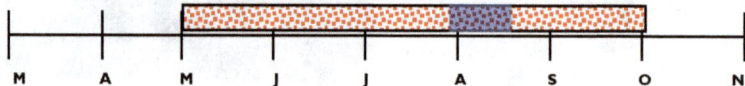

| | | | | | | | | |
|M|A|M|J|J|A|S|O|N|

Host: Dandelion and plantain

Identification: There is no confusing this moth, with 'dirty' orange forewings and bright orange hindwings. Yet another reason to let your dandelions live!

8129 - *Pyrrharctia isabella*
Isabella Tiger Moth

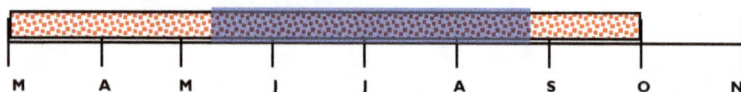

| | | | | | | | | |
|M|A|M|J|J|A|S|O|N|

Host: A wide variety of plants

Identification: Forewings are golden with a few black spots. Abdomen is yellow with black spots. The caterpillar for this species is the official Wooly Bear.

8134 - *Spilosoma congrua*
Agreeable Tiger Moth

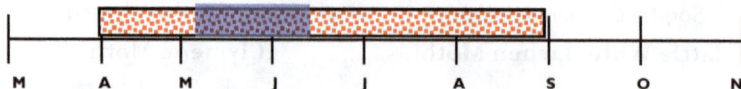

| | | | | | | | | |
|M|A|M|J|J|A|S|O|N|

Host: Dandelion and plantain

Identification: Note that the antennae shafts on this moth are white. The very similar Fall Webworm has black antennae shafts. The bases of the front legs are yellow-orange (not visible in this image).

8111 - *Haploa lecontei*
Leconte's Haploa

8124 - *Virbia immaculata*
Immaculate Holomelina Moth

8129 - *Pyrrharctia isabella*
Isabella Tiger Moth

8134 - *Spilosoma congrua*
Agreeable Tiger Moth

8140 - *Hyphantria cunea*
Fall Webworm Moth

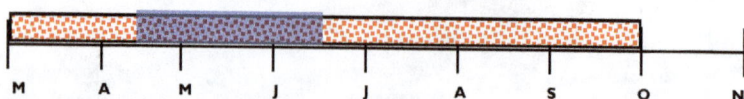

| M | A | M | J | J | A | S | O | N |

Host: Many deciduous trees and shrubs

Identification: In our area this moth is completely white. The caterpillars form communal nests at the ends of tree branches. At Butterfly Ridge, frequently it is Sourwood that houses these nests. The adult Fall Webworm looks very similar to Agreeable Tiger Moth and Virginian Tiger Moth.

....

8146 - *Hypercompe scribonia*
Giant Leopard Moth

| M | A | M | J | J | A | S | O | N |

Host: Many species of plants

Identification: The large black spots on the white background is very unique. Some of the spots are filled with a brilliant blue. The legs and antennae are also blue. The largest of our tiger moths. The caterpillar looks very similar to the Wooly Bear, the name given to the larva of the Isabella Tiger Moth.

8140 – *Hyphantria cunea*
Fall Webworm Moth

8146 – *Hypercompe scribonia*
Giant Leopard Moth

Apantesis sp.

The *Apantesis* group of Tiger Moths can be extremely difficult to distinguish from one another and usually requires a good photograph of the color and banding pattern of the hindwing. The forewing pattern of each species is extremely variable, with different species nearly matching each other.

8169 - *Apantesis phalerata*
Harnessed Tiger Moth

M	A	M	J	J	A	S	O	N

Host: Clover, grasses, dandelion, and plantain

Identification: The hindwings will be yellow/salmon with minimal black banding along the lower margin. The two black spots on the head separate Harnessed Tiger from Nais Tiger which lacks the spots.

8171 - *Apantesis nais*
Nais Tiger Moth

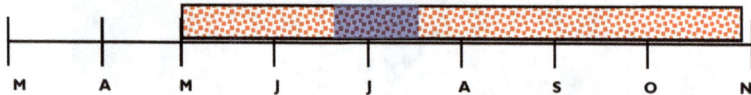

M	A	M	J	J	A	S	O	N

Host: Clover, plantain, violets and grasses

Identification: The hindwings will be yellow/salmon/red with more substantial black marginal banding.

8169 – *Apantesis phalerata*
Harnessed Tiger Moth

8171 - *Apantesis nais*
Nais Tiger Moth

8203 - *Halysidota tessellaris*
Banded Tussock Moth

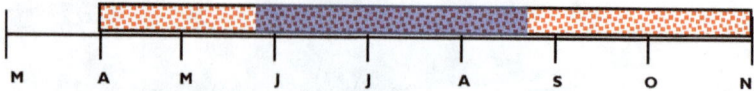

| M | A | M | J | J | A | S | O | N |

Host: Several deciduous tree species
Identification: Note the blue lines behind the head along with multiple gray bands on the forewings. In southeast Ohio, Sycamore Tussock is fairly common and virtually impossible to distinguish from Banded Tussock.

8211 - *Lophocampa caryae*
Hickory Tussock Moth

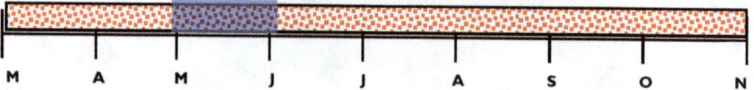

| M | A | M | J | J | A | S | O | N |

Host: Hickory and several other deciduous tree species
Identification: Look for the silvery spots on the golden-brown forewings. During the month of May, this is the most abundant moth at Butterfly Ridge, coming to the sheet by the hundreds.

8230 - *Cycnia tenera*
Delicate Cycnia Moth

| M | A | M | J | J | A | S | O | N |

Host: Milkweed and Dogbane
Identification: The white forewings with a lemon yellow leading edge is very unique among our moths.

8203 - *Halysidota tessellaris*
Banded Tussock Moth

8211 - *Lophocampa caryae*
Hickory Tussock Moth

8230 – *Cycnia tenera*
Delicate Cycnia Moth

8238 - *Euchaetes egle*
Milkweed Tussock Moth

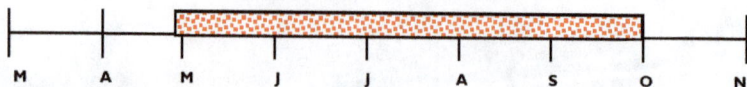

```
M       A       M       J       J       A       S       O       N
```

Host: Milkweed and dogbane

Identification: This is a relatively bland moth, with unmarked gray wings. The body has yellow striping and frequently there is yellow near the head. We have never had a sighting of an adult at Butterfly Ridge, despite countless sightings of the caterpillars.

8267 - *Cisseps fulvicollis*
Yellow-collared Scape Moth

```
M       A       M       J       J       A       S       O       N
```

Host: Grasses, spike rush, and lichens

Identification: This moth is a wasp mimic. Note the colorful collar. This species looks very similar to Grapeleaf Skeletonizer (Hodges #4624) but that species typical has a conspicuous tuft of hairs at the end of the abdomen.

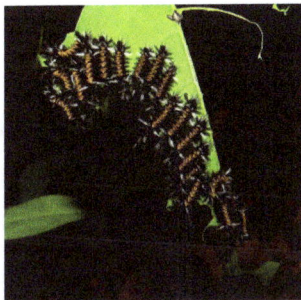

8238 - Euchaetes egle
Milkweed Tussock Moth

8267 - Cisseps fulvicollis
Yellow-collared Scape Moth

Lymantriidae - Tussock Moths

The name "Tussock" is derived from the groupings of hairs on the caterpillars. These groups take the appearance of a tussock, hence the name. Many caterpillars of this group have stinging hairs that are concealed by long hairs. The moths in this group tend to be poorly marked. Several species in this group have flightless females. The best known member of the group is the Gypsy Moth.

8294 - *Dasychira vagans*
Variable Tussock Moth

M	A	M	J	J	A	S	O	N

Host: A wide variety of broad leaved plants

Identification: This moth has a large reniform spot, frequently surrounded by a lighter base color. There is also a subtle 'mask' through the middle of the forewings.

8316 - *Orgyia leucostigma*
White-marked Tussock Moth

M	A	M	J	J	A	S	O	N

Host: Several species of woody plants

Identification: The consistent identification mark to look for on this species is the white spot on each forewing. The female of this species is flightless.

8294 - *Dasychira vagans*
Variable Tussock Moth

Male

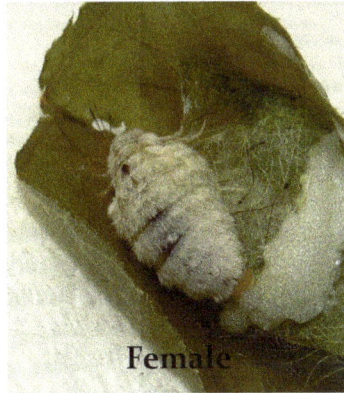

Female

8316 - *Orgyia leucostigma*
White-marked Tussock Moth

Noctuidae - Owlet Moths

The Owlet Moths are the largest family of moths in our area and contain the moths people frequently refer to as 'millers'. While their wing patterns can vary widely they are frequently various shades of gray and brown. Reniform spots, bean-shaped spots in the middle of the forewing, are very common among this group.

8322 - *Idia americalis*
American Idia Moth

M	A	M	J	J	A	S	O	N

Host: Lichens

Identification: This is species looks very much like the next, Common Idia, including the orange-brown reniform spot. The American Idia has bolder dark marks on the leading margin of the forewing.

8323 - *Idia aemula*
Common Idia Moth

M	A	M	J	J	A	S	O	N

Host: Dead leaves

Identification: This is a relatively non-descript moth. Look for the pale reniform spot against the darker pattern of the forewing.

8326 - *Idia rotundalis*
Rotund Idia Moth

M	A	M	J	J	A	S	O	N

Host: Dead leaves and coral fungus

Identification: This moth is very dark. The light colored reniform spot and 'mask' are frequently very subtle to not present.

8322 - *Idia americalis*
American Idia Moth

8323 - *Idia aemula*
Common Idia Moth

8326 - *Idia rotundalis*
Rotund Idia Moth

8329 - *Idia lubricalis*
Glossy Black Idia Moth

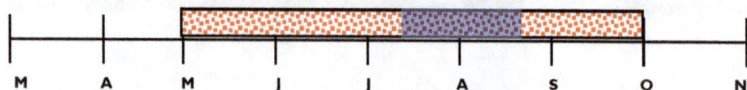

| M | A | M | J | J | A | S | O | N |

Host: Dead leaves, rotting wood, and lichen

Identification: This Idia has the same basic markings as the others. However, the lines and bands are typically white or cream on a very dark background.

8340 - *Zanclognatha lituralis*
Lettered Zanclognatha Moth

| M | A | M | J | J | A | S | O | N |

Host: Dead leaves

Identification: The three dark marginal spots on the forewing, in combination with the chevron in the middle of the wing are distinctive for this species. Similar to the Three-spotted Fillip (Hodges #7647) but the Fillip lacks the center chevron.

8345 - *Zanclognatha laevigata*
Variable Zanclognatha Moth

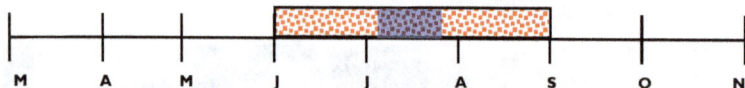

| M | A | M | J | J | A | S | O | N |

Host: Dead leaves

Identification: The chevron in the middle of the forewing is present in this species as well, however it is framed above and below by a broad brown band. This moth resembles Decorated Owlet (Hodges #8490) to a degree.

8329 - *Idia lubricalis*
Glossy Black Idia Moth

8340 - *Zanclognatha*
lituralis
Lettered Zanclognatha
Moth

8345 - *Zanclognatha*
laevigata
Variable Zanclognatha
Moth

8347 - *Zanclognatha obscuripennis*
Dark Zanclognatha Moth

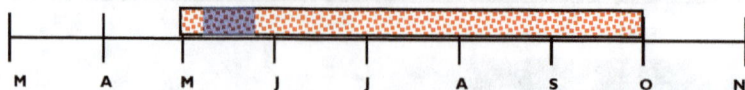

| M | A | M | J | J | A | S | O | N |

Host: Dead leaves

Identification: This Zanclognatha moth has the classic chevron in the middle of the forewing. It also has nearly straight lines above and below the chevron with a wavy at the same level as the chevron.

8353 - *Zanclognatha jacchusalis*
Wavy-lined Zanclognatha Moth

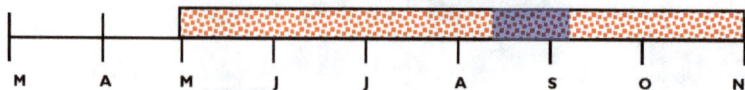

| M | A | M | J | J | A | S | O | N |

Host: Dead leaves

Identification: This Zanclognatha moth has the classic chevron in the middle of the forewing. In addition, two of three lines on the forewing are wavy, compared to the previous species which has one wavy line.

8355 - *Chytolita morbidalis*
Morbid Owlet Moth

| M | A | M | J | J | A | S | O | N |

Host: Dead leaves

Identification: Compared to the Zanclognatha moths, this species has only two forewing lines instead of three. Otherwise very similar.

8370 - *Bleptina caradrinalis*
Bent-winged Owlet Moth

| M | A | M | J | J | A | S | O | N |

Host: Dead leaves

Identification: Look for an indentation in the leading edge of the forewing (black arrow), which is more pronounced in males. The larger black forewing spot (yellow arrow) is also consistent.

8347 - *Zanclognatha obscuripennis*
Dark Zanclognatha Moth

8353 - *Zanclognatha jacchusalis*
Wavy-lined Zanclognatha Moth

8355 - *Chytolita morbidalis*
Morbid Owlet Moth

8370 - *Bleptina caradrinalis*
Bent-winged Owlet Moth

8381 - *Renia discoloralis*
Discolored Renia Moth

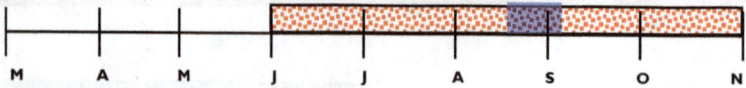

M A M J J A S O N

Host: Dead leaves

Identification: This moth has a unique shape, with the apical portion of the forewing 'fanning' out. This species has the same midwing chevron as the Zanclognatha moths, but also a much smaller spot closer to the point of attachment.

8397 - *Palthis angulalis*
Dark-spotted Palthis Moth

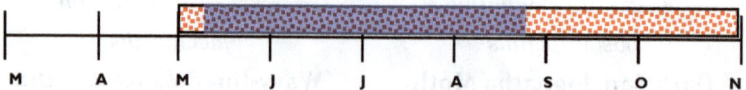

M A M J J A S O N

Host: A wide variety of deciduous and evergreen trees

Identification: In the Dark-spotted Palthis, the middle dark band is not straight but points to the head (yellow arrow). The black arrow indicates the dark spot mentioned in the name.

8398 - *Palthis asopialis*
Faint-spotted Palthis Moth

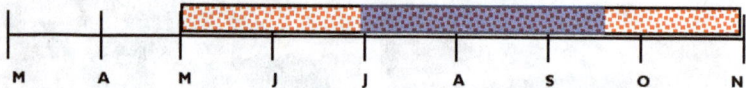

M A M J J A S O N

Host: Oak and beggarticks

Identification: In the Faint-spotted Palthis, the middle dark band is straight. The Faint-spotted has the same dark spot as the Dark-spotted, but there is a white vein going through the middle of the spot.

8381 - *Renia discoloralis*
Discolored Renia Moth

8397 - *Palthis angulalis*
**Dark-spotted Palthis
Moth**

8398 – *Palthis asopialis*
**Faint-spotted Palthis
Moth**

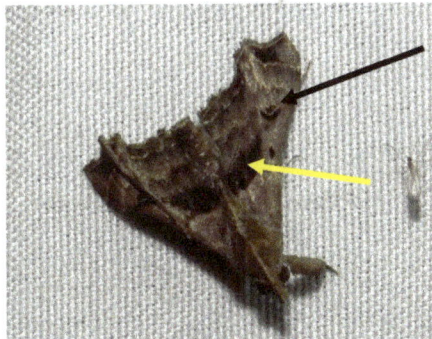

8401 - *Redectis vitrea*
White-spotted Redectis Moth

M	A	M	J	J	A	S	O	N

Host: Crabgrass

Identification: This moth is very unique in having the fan shape forewings, but with a distinct apical notch. The reniform spot is white.

....

8404 - *Rivula propinqualis*
Spotted Grass Moth

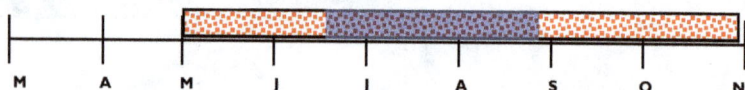

M	A	M	J	J	A	S	O	N

Host: Grasses

Identification: The design on the forewings resembles rams horns, with a dark reniform spot in the curve of the horns.

....

8440 - *Nigetia formosalis*
Thin-winged Owlet Moth

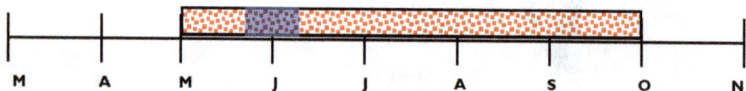

M	A	M	J	J	A	S	O	N

Host: Algae and lichen

Identification: Look for the dark horizontal band crossing a gold-ish background. Little is known about this species.

8401 - *Redectis vitrea*
**White-spotted Redectis
Moth**

8404 - *Rivula propinqualis*
Spotted Grass Moth

8440 – *Nigetia formosalis*
Thin-winged Owlet Moth

Hypena sp.

The *Hypena* genus of Owlet Moths are generally trian-gular in shape with a snout-like projection on the head. They all contain copious amounts of brown in various designs. *Hypena* Moths are typically summer fliers.

8441 - *Hypena manalis*
Flowing-line Bomolocha Moth

M	A	M	J	J	A	S	O	N

Host: False Nettle

Identification: Much like Baltimore Bomolocha except that the post-medial line is smooth and flowing rather than jagged.

8442 - *Hypena baltimoralis*
Baltimore Bomolocha Moth

M	A	M	J	J	A	S	O	N

Host: Maple

Identification: This moth is readily identified by the shape of the solid brown panel on the forewing. Note the brown tab (yellow arrow) extending toward the abdomen and the jagged post medial line (white arrow).

8443 - *Hypena bijugalis*
Dimorphic Bomolocha Moth

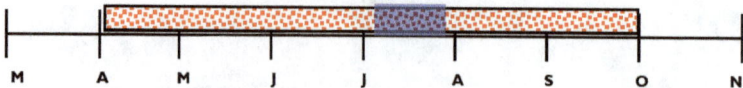

M	A	M	J	J	A	S	O	N

Host: Dogwood

Identification: This moth is sexually dimorphic, meaning male and female look very different. Pictured to the right is the male, relatively non-descript with a pale spot on each forewing. The female looks very similar to the Baltimore Bomolocha except that the post medial line is much less jagged and the brown tab is at the bottom of the brown panel rather than in the middle.

8441 - *Hypena manalis*
**Flowing-line Bomolocha
Moth**

8442 - *Hypena
baltimoralis*
Baltimore Bomolocha

8443 – *Hypena bijugalis*
**Dimorphic Bomolocha
Moth**

8445 - *Hypena abalienalis*
White-lined Bomolocha Moth

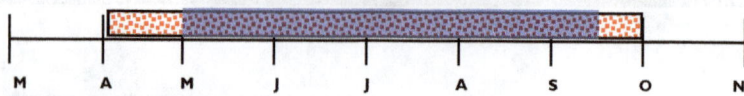

| M | A | M | J | J | A | S | O | N |

Host: Slippery Elm

Identification: The meandering, thick, white post medial line is unique among our Hypena moths.

8446 - *Hypena deceptalis*
Deceptive Bomolocha Moth

| M | A | M | J | J | A | S | O | N |

Host: Unknown in our area

Identification: An obvious, and relatively straight, white line on the forewing separates dark brown from a light brownish-gray.

8447 - *Hypena madefactalis*
Gray-edged Bomolocha Moth

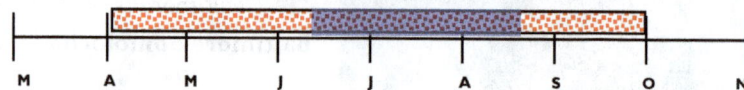

| M | A | M | J | J | A | S | O | N |

Host: Walnut and butternut

Identification: Similar to Deceptive Bomolocha except that the line separating the forewing colors is wavy in this species. The colors on the apical side of the line vary between shades of gray.

8465 - *Hypena scabra*
Green Cloverworm Moth

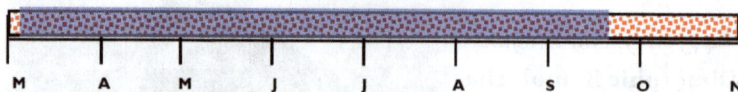

| M | A | M | J | J | A | S | O | N |

Host: Ragweed, clover, beans, and alfalfa

Identification: The forewing designs of the Green Cloverworm Moth can vary greatly, but the one thing they all have in common is a dark horizontal line halfway down the wing.

8445 - *Hypena abalienalis*
White-lined Bomolocha

8446 – *Hypena deceptalis*
Deceptive Bomolocha Moth

8447 - *Hypena madefactalis*
Gray-edged Bomolocha Moth

8465 – *Hypena scabra*
Green Cloverworm Moth

8490 - *Pangrapta decoralis*
Decorated Owlet Moth

M	A	M	J	J	A	S	O	N

Host: Blueberry

Identification: A unique member of the Owlet group, the Decorated Owlet has a scalloped hindwing margin (similar to an Inch-worm Moth). Wings are a complex color scheme of yellows, reds, and browns. Note the reddish 'X' on the forewing.

8499 - *Metalectra discalis*
Common Fungus Moth

M	A	M	J	J	A	S	O	N

Host: Fungi

Identification: This moth can be recognized by the alternating bands of light and dark. Also note the small black dot on the forewing which is consistent across color variations.

8514 - *Scolecocampa liburna*
Deadwood Borer Moth

M	A	M	J	J	A	S	O	N

Host: Decaying logs (or fungi within the logs)

Identification: This moth is a solid straw color with a dark outlined reniform spot and small dark speckles. Also note the dark stripe on the back of the head.

8525 - *Phyprosopus callitrichoides*
Curve-lined Owlet Moth

M	A	M	J	J	A	S	O	N

Host: Greenbriar

Identification: This moth is the ultimate leaf mimic and unlike anything else in our area.

8490 – *Pangrapta decoralis*
Decorated Owlet Moth

8499 - *Metalectra discalis*
Common Fungus Moth

8514 – *Scolecocampa liburna*
Deadwood Borer Moth

8525 - *Phyprosopus callitrichoides*
Curve-lined Owlet Moth

8528 - *Hypsoropha hormos*
Small Necklace Moth

| M | A | M | J | J | A | S | O | N |

Host: Persimmon and sassafras

Identification: The base color of the forewings vary, but the white spots are consistent.

8587 - *Panopoda rufimargo*
Red-lined Panopoda Moth

| M | A | M | J | J | A | S | O | N |

Host: Beech and oak

Identification: Much like Brown Panopoda but the reniform spot is yellow and the head is normally red..

8588 - *Panopoda carneicosta*
Brown Panopoda Moth

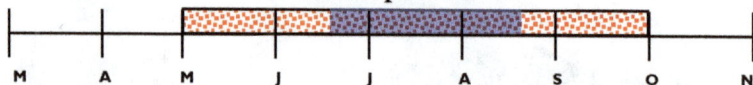

| M | A | M | J | J | A | S | O | N |

Host: Hickory, oak, and willow

Identification: Much like Red-lined Panopoda but the reniform spot is dark and L-shaped. In addition, Brown Panopoda has a dark head, at least when fresh.

8591 - *Phoberia atomaris*
Common Oak Moth

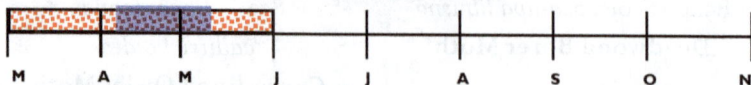

| M | A | M | J | J | A | S | O | N |

Host: Oak

Identification: The reniform spot in this species is dark and obvious. The forewings feature to light colored bands with significant dark shading behind the most apical band.

8528 – *Hypsoropha hormos*
Small Necklace Moth

8587 – *Panopoda rufimargo*
Red-lined Panopoda Moth

8588 – *Panopoda carneicosta*
Brown Panopoda Moth

8591 - *Phoberia atomaris*
Common Oak Moth

8592 - *Cissusa spadix*
Black-dotted Brown Moth

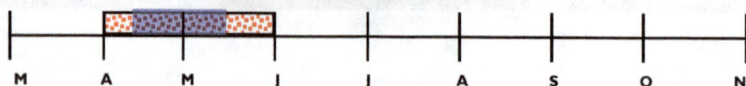

M A M J J A S O N

Host: Oak
Identification: Despite the worn condition of the specimen in the photo, the telltale dark spots in the corner of the forewings are still obvious.

Zale sp.

The Zales are among the most beautiful of the Owlet Moths with bold contrasts of brown, black, white, and yellow in magnificently intricate banding patterns. The wings are scalloped much like an Inch-worm Moth.

8689 - *Zale lunata*
Lunate Zale

M A M J J A S O N

Host: Oak and the Rose Family
Identification: An extremely variable species. About the only consistent attribute to look for is the dark post medial line that extends onto the hindwing (yellow arrow).

8695 - *Zale undularis*
Black Zale

M A M J J A S O N

Host: Black Locust and honeylocust
Identification: This is an extremely dark moth. Note the small yellow reniform spots (yellow arrow).

8592 – *Cissusa spadix*
Black-dotted Brown Moth

8689 - *Zale lunata*
Lunate Zale

8695 – *Zale undularis*
Black Zale

8697 - *Zale minerea*
Colorful Zale

M	A	M	J	J	A	S	O	N

Host: Birch, willow, maple, beech, and white oak.

Identification: Another extremely variable Zale with various shades of brown and inconsistent frosting. The key character to look for is a tooth that extends down from the post medial band (yellow arrow).

8698 - *Zale phaeocapna*

M	A	M	J	J	A	S	O	N

Host: Witchhazel and hazelnut

Identification: An uncommon moth, look for the light patch along the leading edge and very thin, post-medial lines.

8700 - *Zale squamularis*
Gray-banded Zale

M	A	M	J	J	A	S	O	N

Host: Pine

Identification: The broad gray band in the forewing is diagnostic in identifying this moth. While not clearly stated in the research, the data indicates this species may have two broods, a spring brood and a summer brood.

8703 - *Zale duplicata*
Pine False Looper Moth

M	A	M	J	J	A	S	O	N

Host: Eastern White Pine

Identification: The dark band with lighter bands on either side is unique among the Zales. Even still, a great amount of variation is present in this species.

8697 – *Zale minerea*
Colorful Zale Moth

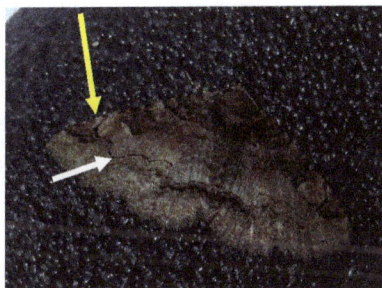

8698 – *Zale phaeocapna*

8700 – *Zale squamularis*
Gray-banded Zale

8703 - *Zale duplicata*
Pine False Looper Moth

8707 - *Zale metatoides*
Washed-out Zale

M	A	M	J	J	A	S	O	N

Host: Pine

Identification: "Washed-out" is a great name for this moth, with wings that feature several subdued shades of brown.

8713.1 - *Zale intenta*
Intent Zale

M	A	M	J	J	A	S	O	N

Host: Cherry and plum

Identification: Look for the black line in the upper portion of the forewing which makes a strong turn toward the head. In addition, a series of small dark lines give the wings a wood-grain look.

8716 - *Zale unilineata*
One-lined Zale

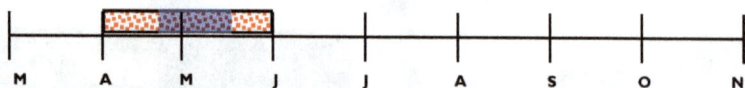

M	A	M	J	J	A	S	O	N

Host: Black Locust

Identification: Look for the narrow yellowish post medial line to identify this moth. Otherwise, this is one of the palest and least marked of the Zales.

8717 - *Zale horrida*
Horrid Zale

M	A	M	J	J	A	S	O	N

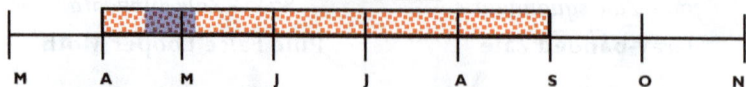

Host: Viburnum

Identification: This Zale is very unique with the light color wings toward the outside and dark toward the inside. The bristly collar is very unique among our Zales.

8707 - *Zale metatoides*
Washed-out Zale

8713.1 – *Zale intenta*
Intent Zale Moth

8716 – *Zale unilineata*
One-lined Zale Moth

8717 – *Zale horrida*
Horrid Zale Moth

8719 - *Euparthenos nubilis*
Locust Underwing Moth

M	A	M	J	J	A	S	O	N

Host: Black Locust

Identification: The orange hindwings with four black bands is unique because of the many black bands. True Underwing moths have only two or three black bands. Also look for the bold white patches on the leading edge of the forewing.

8721 - *Allotria elonympha*
False Underwing Moth

M	A	M	J	J	A	S	O	N

Host: Black Gum, hickory, and walnut

Identification: Look for the black orbicular spot on the forewing, which separates this species from true Underwing Moths. Also notice that the dark band on the hindwing is very even.

8727 - *Parallelia bistriaris*
Maple Looper Moth

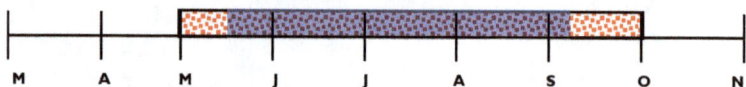

M	A	M	J	J	A	S	O	N

Host: Maple, birch, and walnut

Identification: The Maple Looper has two relatively parallel pale lines on the forewing. There is also varying degrees of frosting on the outer edge of the wings.

8719 – *Euparthenos nubilis*
Locust Underwing Moth

8721 – *Allotria elonympha*
False Underwing Moth

8727 - *Parallelia bistriaris*
Maple Looper Moth

8739 - *Caenurgina erechtea*
Forage Looper Moth

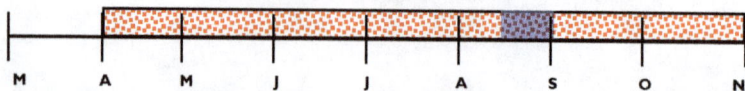

| M | A | M | J | J | A | S | O | N |

Host: Grasses, alfalfa, clover and ragweed

Identification: Notice that the two bands on the forewing do NOT touch and that the basal band (closest to the body) does not reach completely to the wing margin.

8745 - *Mocis texana*
Texas Mocis Moth

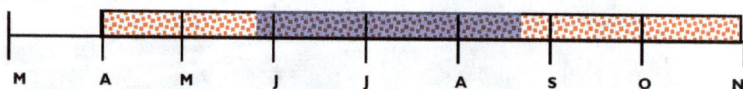

| M | A | M | J | J | A | S | O | N |

Host: Crabgrass

Identification: On the Texas Mocis, the reniform spot (black arrow) on the forewing appears to have a tail (white arrow), giving it a tadpole appearance. Otherwise this species looks like a Panopoda.

8739 - *Caenurgina erechtea*
Forage Looper Moth

8745 – *Mocis texana*
Texas Mocis Moth

Catocala sp. - Underwing Moths

The Underwings are a common group of Owlet Moths that normally fly mid- to late-summer. Some can be quite large and resemble Sphinx Moths. A view of the hindwing, which is frequently covered by the forewings, is essential to the correct identification of moths in this genus.

8771 - *Catocala piatrix*
Penitent Underwing Moth

| M | A | M | J | J | A | S | O | N |

Host: Hickory and walnut

Identification: This Underwing has one very prominent light streak post-medial stripe on the forewing with a second, less obvious one.

8773 - *Catocala epione*
Epione Underwing Moth

| M | A | M | J | J | A | S | O | N |

Host: Hickory

Identification: The Epione Underwing is identified by the light-colored reniform spot on the forewing in combination with the white-fringed, black hindwing.

8778 - *Catocala habilis*
Habilis Underwing Moth

| M | A | M | J | J | A | S | O | N |

Host: Ash, hickory, butternut, and walnut

Identification: This species is sort of non-descript. Look for white-washed bands on the forewings and orange and black striping on the hindwings.

258

8771 - *Catocala piatrix*
Penitent Underwing Moth

8773 – *Catocala epione*
Epione Underwing Moth

8778 – *Catocala habilis*
Habilis Underwing Moth

8779 - *Catocala serena*
Serene Underwing Moth

M   A   M   J   J   A   S   O   N

Host: Hickory and walnut

Identification: Thin dark bands on the forewing with a faint lighter band toward the outer margin. Hindwing yellow and black striped.

8782 - *Catocala flebilis*
Mournful Underwing Moth

M   A   M   J   J   A   S   O   N

Host: Hickory

Identification: The brown reniform spot (yellow arrow) and the dark longitudinal band (white arrow) are the key features of the forewing of this species. Hindwings are black with a white fringe.

8783 - *Catocala angusi*
Angus' Underwing Moth

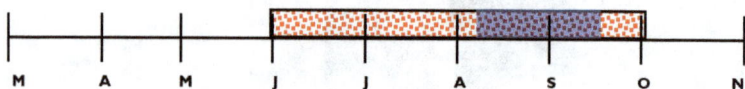

M   A   M   J   J   A   S   O   N

Host: Hickory

Identification: Angus' is much like Mournful Underwing except that the hindwing fringe of Angus' is gray rather than white.

8784 - *Catocala obscura*
Obscure Underwing Moth

M   A   M   J   J   A   S   O   N

Host: Hickory and walnut

Identification: Similar in appearance to Serene Underwing, Obscure has a dark hindwing with pale fringe rather than the tiger striped hindwing of Serene.

8779 - *Catocala serena*
Serene Underwing Moth

8782 - *Catocala flebilis*
Mournful Underwing

8783 – *Catocala angusi*
Angus' Underwing Moth

8784 - *Catocala obscura*
Obscure Underwing Moth

8785 - *Catocala residua*
Residua Underwing Moth

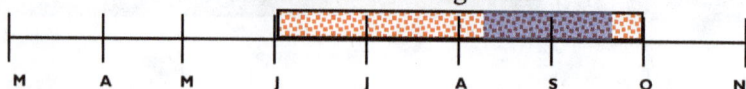

```
M    A    M    J    J    A    S    O    N
```

Host: Hickory

Identification: Residua is much like Obscure, however with a generally darker overall appearance and a dingy hindwing fringe when compared to Obscure.

8788 - *Catocala retecta*
Yellow-gray Underwing Moth

```
M    A    M    J    J    A    S    O    N
```

Host: Hickory and walnut

Identification: The dark longitudinal band common in many Underwings is broken or staggered (white circle) in this species. Also, the white hindwing fringe has a checked appearance (yellow arrow).

8790 - *Catocala dejecta*
Dejected Underwing Moth

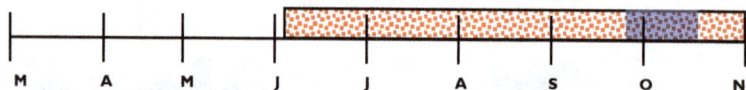

```
M    A    M    J    J    A    S    O    N
```

Host: Hickory and oak

Identification: This Underwing is one of the more easily recognized, having a very distinct light colored patch along the forewing margin. The hindwing is black with a checkered white fringe. The moth in the photo to the right is well worn and has lost it's fringe.

8792 - *Catocala vidua*
Widow Underwing Moth

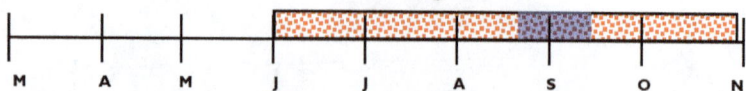

```
M    A    M    J    J    A    S    O    N
```

Host: Hickory, walnut, oak, and black locust

Identification: Widow Underwing is very unique in having two parallel concave bands on the forewings (black arrows).

262

8785 - *Catocala residua*
Residua Underwing Moth

8788 – *Catocala retecta*
**Yellow-gray Underwing
Moth**

8790 – *Catocala dejecta*
Dejected Underwing Moth

8792 - *Catocala vidua*
Widow Underwing Moth

8795 - *Catocala paleogama*
Old-wife Underwing Moth

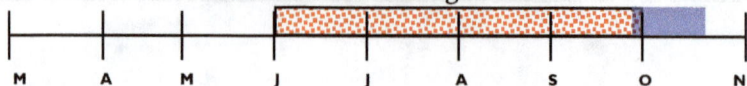

| M | A | M | J | J | A | S | O | N |

Host: Hickory and walnut

Identification: Look for the 'M' made along the inner margin of the forewings. Hindwings orange and black striped.

8796 - *Catocala nebulosa*
Clouded Underwing Moth

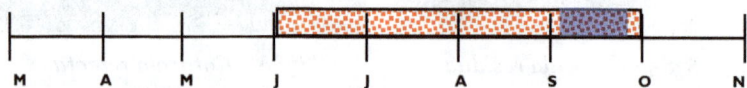

| M | A | M | J | J | A | S | O | N |

Host: Hickory and walnut

Identification: The multi-colored wings of this species is very unique. The upper portion of the forewings is considerably darker than the lower portions of the wings. The hindwings, not shown in photo to the right, are orange and black striped.

8797 - *Catocala subnata*
Youthful Underwing Moth

| M | A | M | J | J | A | S | O | N |

Host: Hickory and walnut

Identification: The specimen pictured to the right is quite worn. The features to look for are the brown reniform spot as well as brown shading on the outer edge of the post-medial band (white arrow).

8795 – *Catocala palaeogama*
Oldwife Underwing Moth

8796 – *Catocala nebulosi*
Clouded Underwing Moth

8797 - *Catocala subnata*
Youthful Underwing

8798 - *Catocala neogama*
Bride Underwing Moth

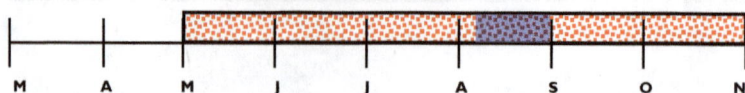

M A M J J A S O N

Host: Hickory, oak, and walnut

Identification: The brown banding and reniform spot are much like Youthful Underwing. However, Bride Underwing has three distinct areas of dark shading in addition (yellow arrows).

8801 - *Catocala ilia*
Ilia Underwing Moth

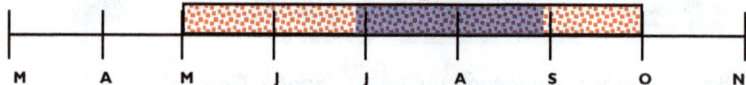

M A M J J A S O N

Host: Oak

Identification: The key identifying feature of Ilia Underwing is that the reniform spot is outlined in white (yellow arrow). The hindwings are orange and black.

8801.1 - *Catocala umbrosa*
Umber Underwing Moth

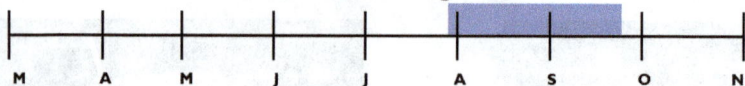

M A M J J A S O N

Host: Oak

Identification: The Umber Underwing was once considered a form of Ilia Underwing. The difference seems to be that in Umber the reniform spot is not outlined in white and that there is a pale band that goes across the forewing. This species is not officially recognized in Ohio.

8798 – *Catocala neogama*
Bride Underwing Moth

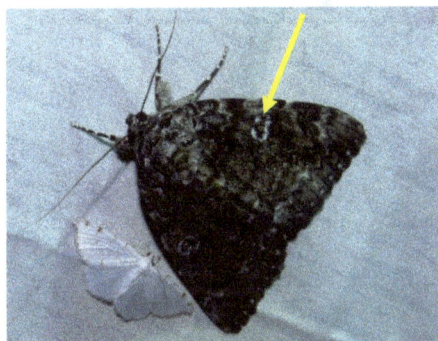

8801 – *Catocala ilia*
Ilia Underwing Moth

8801.1 – *Catocala umbrosa*
Umber Underwing Moth

8802 - *Catocala cerogama*
Yellow-banded Underwing Moth

| M | A | M | J | J | A | S | O | N |

Host: Basswood and red maple

Identification: The forewings of the Yellow-banded have a conspicuous white spot which is distinctive. The hindwing is even more diagnostic with a single yellow band, while most Underwings have multiple colorful bands.

8834 - *Catocala amatrix*
Sweetheart Underwing Moth

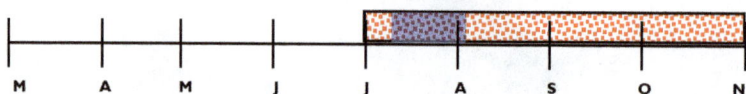

| M | A | M | J | J | A | S | O | N |

Host: Poplar and willow

Identification: The forewing of this moth more closely resembles Angus or Mournful Underwing. However, the hindwing is a beautiful bright red. This species overwinters as an egg.

8849 - *Catocala andromedae*
Andromeda Underwing Moth

| M | A | M | J | J | A | S | O | N |

Host: Blueberry

Identification: The distinctive feature of the Andromeda Underwing is the dark inside margin on the forewing. Also note the conspicuous dark spot next to the margin.

8802 - *Catocala cerogama*
**Yellow-banded
Underwing Moth**

8834 - *Catocala amatrix*
**Sweetheart Underwing
Moth**

8849 - *Catocala andromeda*
**Andromeda Underwing
Moth**

8857 - *Catocala ultronia*
Ultronia Underwing Moth

```
M    A    M    J    J    A    S    O    N
```

Host: Apple and cherry

Identification: The forewings of the Ultronia Underwing have a woodgrain appearance which is unique among the Underwing Moths. Forewing tips are normally a lighter color than the rest of the wing. Hindwings are orange and black.

8864 - *Catocala grynea*
Woody Underwing Moth

```
M    A    M    J    J    A    S    O    N
```

Host: Apple, hawthorn, and plum

Identification: The gray wings with the chocolate brown center is very unique among the underwings. Hindwings are orange and black.

8876 - *Catocala micronympha*
Little Nymph Underwing Moth

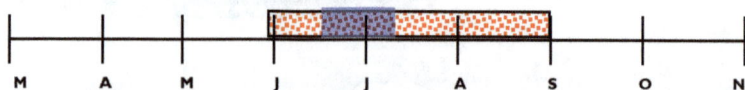

```
M    A    M    J    J    A    S    O    N
```

Host: Oak

Identification: This species is varies wildly in it's appearance. The one consistency is the white edge of the post-medial line (black arrow). Hindwings are orange and black.

8857 – *Catocala ultronia*
**Ultronia Underwing
Moth**

8864 – *Catocala grynea*
Woody Underwing

8876 – Catocala
micronympha
**Little Nymph Underwing
Moth**

8898 - *Allagrapha aerea*
Unspotted Looper Moth

M A M J J A S O N

Host: Soybean, stinging nettle, and the Sunflower Family
Identification: Wing shape and the tufts of hair on the back confirm this as a Looper. The yellow head and unmarked wings are distinctive of Unspotted Looper.

8908 - *Anagrapha precationis*
Common Looper Moth

M A M J J A S O N

Host: A wide variety of herbaceous plants
Identification: The silver spot on the forewing can vary in shape but generally resembles a figure-eight, appearing to be comprised of two separate, but sometimes touching, pieces. Celery Looper has a single silver piece.

8924 - *Autographa falcifera*
Celery Looper Moth

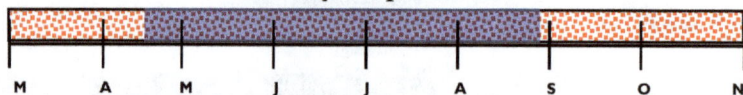

M A M J J A S O N

Host: Viburnum and garden vegetables
Identification: The silver spot on the forewing appears to be a single, elongated spot. Common Looper appears to have two individual spots sometimes joined to make a figure-eight.

8898 - *Allagrapha aerea*
Unspotted Looper Moth

8908 - *Anagrapha precationis*
Common Looper Moth

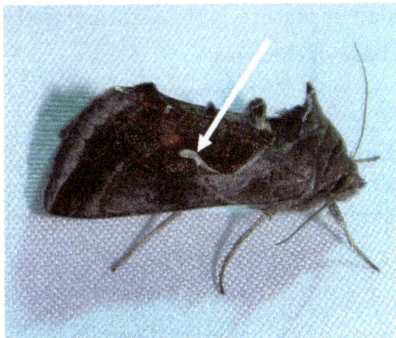

8924 - *Autographa falcifera*
Celery Looper Moth

8955 - *Marathyssa inficita*
Dark Marathyssa Moth

M — A — M — J — J — A — S — O — N

Host: Poison ivy and sumacs

Identification: Sort of the stealth bomber of the moth world, with wings folded like an accordion at rest.

8957 - *Paectes oculatrix*
Eyed Paectes Moth

M — A — M — J — J — A — S — O — N

Host: Poison ivy

Identification: The large eyespots and the forewing tips are very unique among Butterfly Ridge's moths. If only they would eat up more of our poison ivy!

8959 - *Paectes pygmaea*
Pygmy Paectes Moth

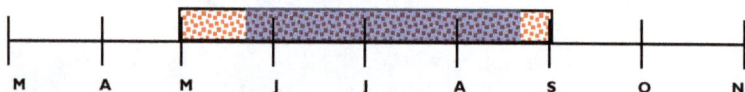

M — A — M — J — J — A — S — O — N

Host: Winged sumac

Identification: This moth can vary in color from greenish to brown to almost red. The consistent feature is the light colored spot on each forewing near the base of the wing.

8968 - *Eutelia pulcherrimus*
Beautiful Eutelia Moth

M — A — M — J — J — A — S — O — N

Host: Poison ivy

Identification: The varying shades of red, gold, and brown with the "stealth-bomber" appearance is unlike any moth in our area.

8955 - *Marathyssa inficita*
Dark Marathyssa Moth

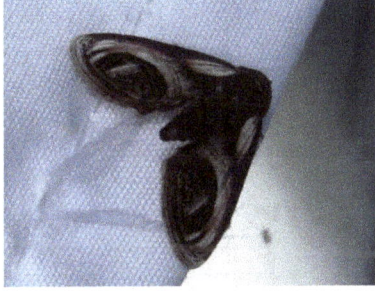

8957 – *Paectes oculatrix*
Eyed Paectes Moth

8959 - *Paectes pygmaea*
Pygmy Paectes Moth

8968 – *Eutelia pulcherrimus*
Beautiful Eutelia Moth

8983 - *Meganola minuscula*
Confused Meganola Moth

```
M   A   M   J   J   A   S   O   N
```

Host: Beech, oak, and willow

Identification: This is a rather bland little moth. The only meaningful marking is an "eyeglasses" shaped post-medial line. This moth differs from the Costal Plain Meganola in lacking conspicuous marginal spots on the forewing.

8983.1 - *Meganola phylla*
Costal Plain Meganola Moth

```
M   A   M   J   J   A   S   O   N
```

Host: Oak

Identification: This moth has the same "eyeglasses" as above, but also has two consistent spots on the margin of each forewing. Some researchers believe these two species to actually be the same moth.

9025 - *Oruza albocostaliata*
White Edge Moth

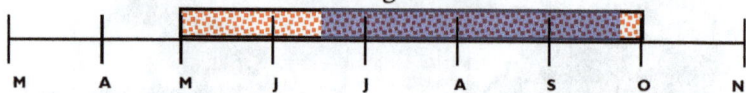

```
M   A   M   J   J   A   S   O   N
```

Host: Unknown

Identification: This moth is very recognizable by the white, leading edge of the forewing. The pair of white lines in the wings are reminiscent of some of the emeralds.

9044 - *Marimatha nigrofimbria*
Black-bordered Lemon Moth

```
M   A   M   J   J   A   S   O   N
```

Host: Crabgrass

Identification: Look for bright yellow wings with black fringe.

8983 - *Meganola minuscula*
Confused Meganola Moth

8983.1 - *Meganola phylla*
Costal Plain Meganola Moth

9025 - *Oruza albocostaliata*
White Edge Moth

9044 - *Marimatha nigrofimbria*
Black Bordered Lemon Moth

9047 - *Protodeltote muscosula*
Large Mossy Lithacodia Moth

| M | A | M | J | J | A | S | O | N |

Host: The only listing available is an ambiguous reference to "Swamp Grasses".

Identification: Note the totem face on the wings, with two eyes and a mouth!

9049 - *Maliattha synochitis*
Black-dotted Lithacodia Moth

| M | A | M | J | J | A | S | O | N |

Host: Knotweed

Identification: The green 'shield' in the center of the wings is very unique. There are also black dots on either side of the shield.

9051 - *Lithacodia musta*
Small Mossy Lithacodia Moth

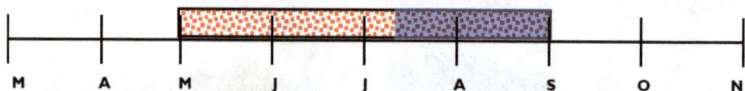

| M | A | M | J | J | A | S | O | N |

Host: Unknown

Identification: The totem face on this moth is not as obvious as on Large Mossy. The reniform spots are more prominent here.

9053 - *Pseudeustrotia carneola*
Pink-barred Lithacodia Moth

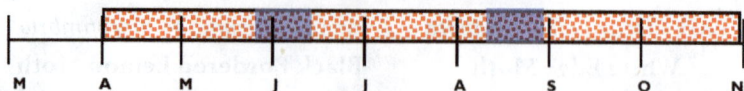

| M | A | M | J | J | A | S | O | N |

Host: Dock, smartweed, and goldenrod

Identification: Technically, the diagonal bands across the forewings are considered to be a pale pink. They are so pale of pink, white would seem to be a better description, however it is a unique design among our Butterfly Ridge moths.

9047 - *Protodeltote muscosula*
Large Mossy Lithacodia Moth

9049 - *Maliattha synochitis*
Black-dotted Lithacodia Moth

9051 - *Lithacodia musta*
Small Mossy Lithacodia Moth

9053 – *Pseudeustrotia carneola*
Pink-barred Lithacodia Moth

9062 - *Cerma cerintha*
Tuft Bird-dropping Moth

M   A   M   J   J   A   S   O   N

Host: Fruit trees

Identification: Hopefully the reason for the common name is obvious. This moth does bear some resemblance to the previous moth with some reversal of dark and light patches.

9065 - *Leuconycta diphteroides*
Green Leuconycta Moth

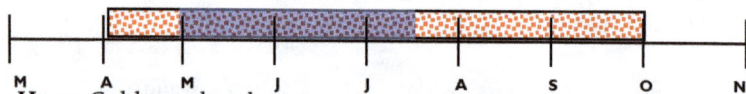

M   A   M   J   J   A   S   O   N

Host: Goldenrod and aster

Identification: The dark patch on the leading edge of the forewing is distinctive among our green Owlet Moths.

9066 - *Leuconycta lepidula*
Marbled-green Leuconycta Moth

M   A   M   J   J   A   S   O   N

Host: Dandelion

Identification: This moth has a black base color with several large green spots. Moth of the other green Owlet moths have a green base color with dark spotting.

9095 - *Ponometia erastrioides*
Small Bird-dropping Moth

M   A   M   J   J   A   S   O   N

Host: Ragweed

Identification: This moth is white with some dark markings on the outer half of the forewing. Looks similar to Schlaeger's Fruitworm Moth (Hodges #1011) which has more extensive dark markings.

9062 - *Cerma cerintha*
Tuft Bird-dropping Moth

9065 - *Leuconycta diphteroides*
Green Leuconycta Moth

9066 - *Leuconycta lepidula*
Marbled-green Leuconycta Moth

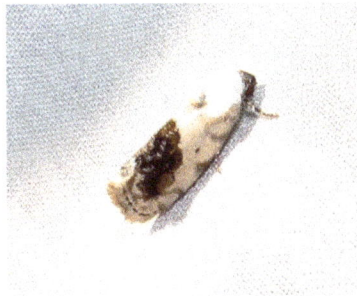

9095 - *Ponometia erastrioides*
Small Bird-dropping Moth

9127 - *Spragueia leo*
Common Spragueia Moth

M   A   M   J   J   A   S   O   N

Host: Bindweed and ragweed

Identification: The Halloween colors on this moth are very unique. This is a small moth, resembling a Leafroller more than an Owlet.

9177 - *Panthea acronyctoides*
Black Zigzag Moth

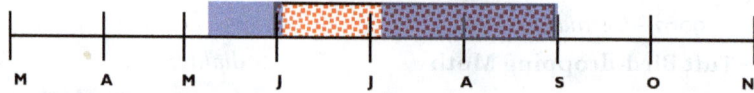

M   A   M   J   J   A   S   O   N

Host: Hemlock and pine

Identification: Zigzag is an appropriate description for the black lines that run horizontally across the white forewings.

9182 - *Panthea furcilla*
Eastern Panthea Moth

M   A   M   J   J   A   S   O   N

Host: Pine

Identification: This species is similar to the Zigzag but the lines are straighter and the base color is gray rather than white. This species has two generations each year.

9127 - *Spragueia leo*
Common Spragueia Moth

9177 – *Panthea acronyctoides*
Black Zigzag Moth

9182 - *Panthea furcilla*
Eastern Panthea Moth

9184 - *Calocasia flavicornis*
Yellowhorn Moth

M A M J J A S O N

Host: Beech, elm, maple, oak and others
Identification: This moth is easily recognized by the dark gray central shield on the light gray wings. The antennae are also yellow, hence the common name. This species has two generations.

9185 - *Calocasia propinquilinea*
Closebanded Yellowhorn Moth

M A M J J A S O N

Host: Mainly on birch but other deciduous trees as well
Identification: This Yellowhorn has the characteristic yellow antennae, but the dark gray shield from the above species is now more of a subtle, tooth-edged mask on the wings.

9189 - *Charadra deridens*
Laugher Moth

M A M J J A S O N

Host: Beech, birch, maple, and oak
Identification: The common name for this moth is a bit of a mystery. Identification is a bit simpler however if you look for the large 'eye' on each forewing.

9193 - *Raphia frater*
Brother Moth

M A M J J A S O N

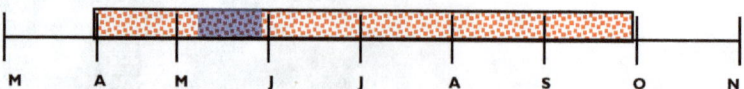

Host: Birch, cottonwood, willow, and alder
Identification: This species has a shield similar to Yellowhorn but with two conspicuous forewing spots.

9184 - *Calocasia flavicornis*
Yellowhorn Moth

9185 - *Calocasia propinquilinea*
**Closebanded Yellowhorn
Moth**

9189 - *Charadra deridens*
Laugher Moth

9193 - *Raphia frater*
Brother Moth

Acronicta sp. - Dagger Moths

The Dagger Moths are generally gray in color with heavy black lines that run longitudinally through the forewing. These black lines are the 'daggers'.

....

9200 - *Acronicta americana*
American Dagger Moth

M	A	M	J	J	A	S	O	N

Host: A wide variety of deciduous trees

Identification: The 'daggers' that this group is known for are not present on this species. Instead look for a row of white chevrons. The caterpillar is densely hairy with long yellow-white hairs.

....

9207 - *Acronicta innotata*
Unmarked Dagger Moth

M	A	M	J	J	A	S	O	N

Host: Hickory, birch, cherry, and willow

Identification: The pattern of the post-medial line on the solid pale gray background is very unique. This moth is very common on summer nights.

....

9209 - *Acronicta radcliffei*
Radcliffe's Dagger Moth

M	A	M	J	J	A	S	O	N

Host: Cherry, apple, and hawthorn

Identification: The post-medial line is much like that of Unmarked Dagger. Look for the shield-shaped patch just behind the head. This is one of our smaller Daggers.

9200 - *Acronicta americana*
American Dagger Moth

9207 – *Acronicta innotata*
Unmarked Dagger Moth

9209 – *Acronicta radcliffei*
Radcliffe's Dagger Moth

9221 - *Acronicta funeralis*
Funerary Dagger Moth

M	A	M	J	J	A	S	O	N

Host: A wide variety of deciduous trees

Identification: An especially beautiful Dagger. The inside margins of the forewings are dark shaded, creating a long dark rectangle when the wings are closed. Also note the dark triangle near the reniform spot.

9225 - *Acronicta vinnula*
Delightful Dagger Moth

M	A	M	J	J	A	S	O	N

Host: Elm

Identification: Delightful Dagger is recognized by several features. First of all, each forewing features two 'daggers' (black arrows), one along the edge of the thorax, the other near the trailing edge of the forewing. Also note the straight section of the post-medial line near the trailing edge (red arrow).

9229 - *Acronicta hasta*
Speared Dagger Moth

M	A	M	J	J	A	S	O	N

Host: Cherry, oak, and plum

Identification: Note that there are four daggers on each forewing, most of which are forked or branched.

9221 - *Acronicta funeralis*
Funerary Dagger Moth

9225 - *Acronicta vinnula*
Delightful Dagger Moth

9229 – *Acronicta hasta*
Speared Dagger Moth

9235 - *Acronicta spinigera*
Nondescript Dagger Moth

| M | A | M | J | J | A | S | O | N |

Host: Unknown

Identification: This species looks similar to American Dagger but has a prominent reniform spot and circular spot on each forewing. This moth has three 'daggers', only two of which are visible in the photo on the opposite page.

9237 - *Acronicta interrupta*
Interrupted Dagger Moth

| M | A | M | J | J | A | S | O | N |

Host: Several deciduous tree species

Identification: Forewing spots on this Dagger are very subtle but it does have two conspicuous daggers on each forewing.

9241 - *Acronicta fragilis*
Fragile Dagger Moth

| M | A | M | J | J | A | S | O | N |

Host: Apple, birch, plum, willow, and spruce

Identification: This moth has a showy display of zigzag black lines on a white background. On the back of the thorax is a design that could be easily recognized as a skull.

9241.1 - *Acronicta heitzmani*
Heitzman's Dagger Moth

| M | A | M | J | J | A | S | O | N |

Host: Apple, Birch, Plum, Willow, and Spruce

Identification: This moth looks like a smaller, discolored version of Fragile Dagger. Many of these same markings but with a sandy base color.

9235 - *Acronicta spinigera*
Nondescript Dagger Moth

9237 - *Acronicta interrupta*
Interrupted Dagger Moth

9241 - *Acronicta fragilis*
Fragile Dagger Moth

9241.1 - *Acronicta heitzmani*
Heitzman's Dagger Moth

9243 - *Acronicta ovata*
Ovate Dagger Moth

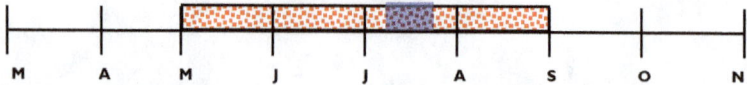

| M | A | M | J | J | A | S | O | N |

Host: Beech, birch, and oak

Identification: This species has a harness design toward the base of the forewings (black arrow) and three sets of large circular spots (white arrows).

9247 - *Acronicta tristis*

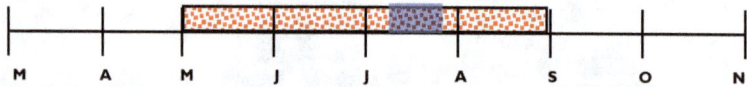

| M | A | M | J | J | A | S | O | N |

Host: Beech

Identification: This species is much like Ovate Dagger but is generally a more salt and pepper color (less brown) and the reniform spot is very subtle.

9249 - *Acronicta increta*
Southern Oak Dagger Moth

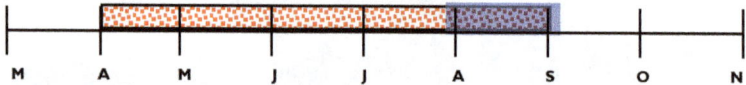

| M | A | M | J | J | A | S | O | N |

Host: Oak

Identification: Much like the previous two species, with three sets of spots and a harness looking design near the forewing base. This species has dark shading near the apex of the forewing.

9254 - *Acronicta afflicta*
Afflicted Dagger Moth

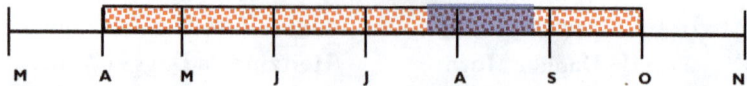

| M | A | M | J | J | A | S | O | N |

Host: Oak

Identification: This moth is very dark, with conspicuous white eyes, sort of like Wilson in the Cast Away movie.

9243 - *Acronicta ovata*
Ovate Dagger Moth

9247 - *Acronicta tristis*

9249 - *Acronicta increta*
Southern Oak Dagger Moth

9254 - *Acronicta afflicta*
Afflicted Dagger Moth

9259 - *Acronicta noctivaga*
Night-Wandering Dagger Moth

| M | A | M | J | J | A | S | O | N |

Host: Poplar

Identification: This species is a collection of alternating black and white markings. A subtle spot, which seems to be consistent, is a black chevron on the forewing margin.

9266 - *Acronicta lithospila*
Streaked Dagger Moth

| M | A | M | J | J | A | S | O | N |

Host: Oak and hickory

Identification: This moth is aptly named, as the gray and brown streaking on the wings is unlike our other moths. The Three-lined Balsa (Hodges# 9663) is superficially similar but is easily distinguished by the three marginal lines on the forewing.

9281 - *Acronicta fallax*
Green Marvel

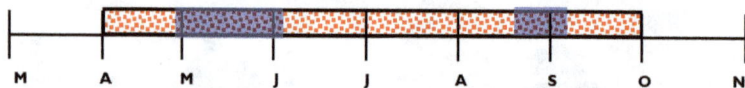

| M | A | M | J | J | A | S | O | N |

Host: Viburnum

Identification: This moth is easily recognized by the green base color with black chevrons scattered throughout.

9259 - *Acronicta noctivaga*
Night-Wandering Dagger Moth

9266 - *Acronicta lithospila*
Streaked Dagger Moth

9281 - *Acronicta fallax*
Green Marvel

9285 - *Polygrammate hebraeicum*
The Hebrew

```
M    A    M    J    J    A    S    O    N
```

Host: Black Gum

Identification: The black and white pattern on the forewings is very distinctive.   Closest in resemblance would be the Black Zigzag Moth, but notice that the Hebrew's marks are not connected to form a line.

9301 - *Eudryas grata*
Beautiful Wood Nymph

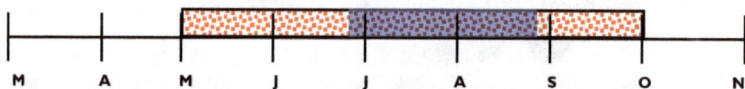

```
M    A    M    J    J    A    S    O    N
```

Host: Grape, Hops, and Virginia Creeper

Identification: The bold white band is unlike any other moth that flies at Butterfly Ridge.

9309 - *Psychomorpha epimenis*
Grapevine Epimenis Moth

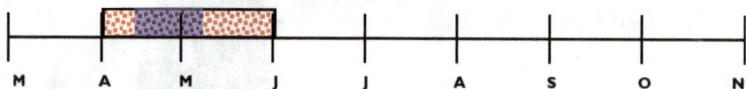

```
M    A    M    J    J    A    S    O    N
```

Host: Grape

Identification: This moth is primarily diurnal or day-flying. The combination of white, black, and red is very unique among moths or butterflies.

9314 - *Alypia octomaculata*
Eight-spotted Forester Moth

```
M    A    M    J    J    A    S    O    N
```

Host: Grape and Virginia Creeper

Identification: This is another day-flying moth. Look for two large white spots on each wing plus fuzzy orange legs.

9285 - *Polygrammate hebraeicum*
The Hebrew

9301 - *Eudryas grata*
Beautiful Wood Nymph

9309 - *Psychomorpha epimenis*
Grapevine Epimenis Moth

9314 - *Alypia octomaculata*
Eight-spotted Forester Moth

9410 - Neoligia crytora

| | | | | | | | | |
|M|A|M|J|J|A|S|O|N|

Host: Unknown

Identification: The two-tone pattern of the wings is distinctive, with brown on the basal end and white frosted on the apical end. The two small dark boxes in the frosting is also diagnostic.

9427 - *Meropleon diversicolor*
Multicolored Sedgeminer Moth

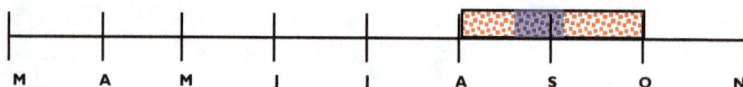

| | | | | | | | | |
|M|A|M|J|J|A|S|O|N|

Host: Sedges

Identification: This mouth is sort of a mix of a Paectes and a Looper. The teardrop-shape spot near the base of the forewing is similar to that of Pygmy Paectes while another forewing spot is similar to the silvery spot on some of the Loopers.

9479 - *Papaipema lysimachiae*
Loosestrife Borer Moth

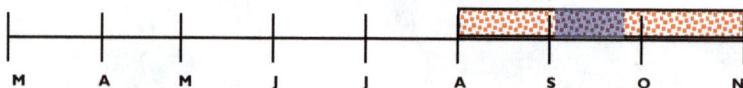

| | | | | | | | | |
|M|A|M|J|J|A|S|O|N|

Host: Loosestrife

Identification: The silver spots on the wings are similar to that of a necklace moth but there is an obvious space separating the spots of each forewing.

9483 - *Papaipema inquaesita*
Sensitive Fern Borer Moth

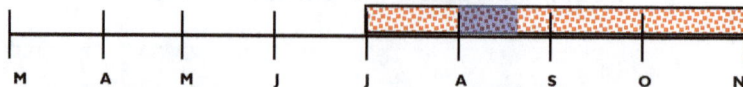

| | | | | | | | | |
|M|A|M|J|J|A|S|O|N|

Host: Sensitive fern

Identification: The 'W' shape on the forewings makes this moth easy to recognize.

298

9410 - Neoligia crytora

9427 - *Meropleon diversicolor*
Multicolored Sedgeminer Moth

9479 – *Papaipema lysimachiae*
Loosestrife Borer Moth

9483 - *Papaipema inquaesita*
Sensitive Fern Borer Moth

9485 - *Papaipema baptisiae*
Indigo Stem Borer Moth

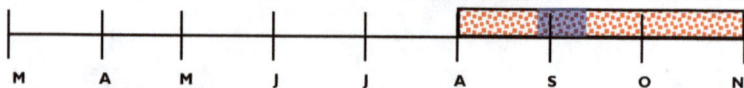

|M|A|M|J|J|A|S|O|N|

Host: Wild indigo and dogbane

Identification: This is a beautiful moth, very similar to Loose-strife Borer (Hodges# 9479). Indigo Stem Borer features showy white spots and the edge of the reniform spot of the forewing.

9547 - *Phlogophora periculosa*
Brown Angle Shades Moth

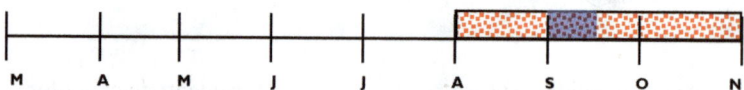

|M|A|M|J|J|A|S|O|N|

Host: Hickory, birch, cherry, and willow

Identification: Somewhat similar to *Hypena* (Hodges #8442). In the Angle Shades, the brown patch does not reach the leading edge of the forewing, unlike *Hypena*.

9618 - *Phosphila turbulenta*
Turbulent Phosphila Moth

|M|A|M|J|J|A|S|O|N|

Host: Greenbriar

Identification: This moth is the classic little brown moth seen at porch lights. Distinctive features are few. Note the white medial line, with dark brown on the basal side of the line, and light brown on the apical side of the line. Contrary to the adult, the caterpillar is very showy and feeds gregariously on Greenbriar, which can be a nuisance plant in midwestern woodlots.

9485 - *Papaipema baptisiae*
Indigo Stem Borer Moth

9547 - *Phlogophora periculosa*
Brown Angle Shades Moth

9618 - *Phosphila turbulenta*
Turbulent Phosphila Moth

9630 - *Callopistria floridensis*
Florida Fern Moth

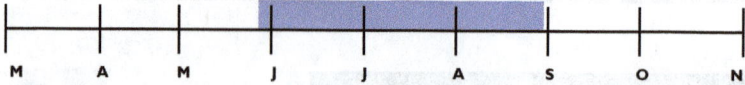

| M | A | M | J | J | A | S | O | N |

Host: Ferns

Identification: This moth bears a strong resemblance to Brown Angle Shades, however in this species the dark brown on the forewing extends completely to the margin.

··

9650 - *Athetis tarda*
Slowpoke Moth

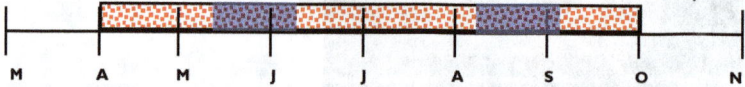

| M | A | M | J | J | A | S | O | N |

Host: Oak

Identification: The Slowpoke is a non-descript moth without any distinctive markings. The common name is derived from the lethargic nature of it's caterpillar.

··

9662 - *Balsa malana*
Many-dotted Appleworm Moth

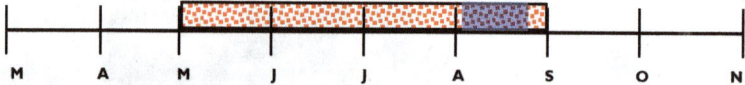

| M | A | M | J | J | A | S | O | N |

Host: Apple, cherry, elm, plum, and pear

Identification: This moth is similar to the Three-lined Balsa but without the streaking on the forewings.

··

9663 - *Balsa tristrigella*
Three-lined Balsa Moth

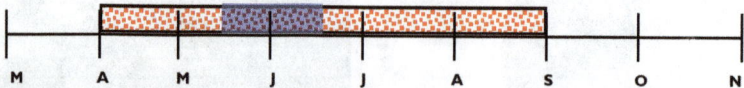

| M | A | M | J | J | A | S | O | N |

Host: Hawthorn

Identification: The "three lines" are indicated with arrows. The rest of the forewing is streaked. A rare moth at Butterfly Ridge.

9630 - *Callopistria floridensis*
Florida Fern Moth

9650 - *Athetis tarda*
Slowpoke Moth

9662 - *Balsa malana*
Many-dotted Appleworm Moth

9663 - *Balsa tristrigella*
Three-lined Balsa Moth

9669 - *Spodoptera ornithogalli*
Yellow-striped Armyworm Moth

M	A	M	J	J	A	S	O	N

Host: Many herbaceous plants including grasses and vegetables

Identification: Only the darts come remotely close to the intricate designs of bold lines and subtle frosting that the Armyworm displays. The 'yellow-stripe' is actually a feature of the caterpillar, although the adult has a golden stripe on the forewing as well.

9684 - *Elaphria grata*
Grateful Midget Moth

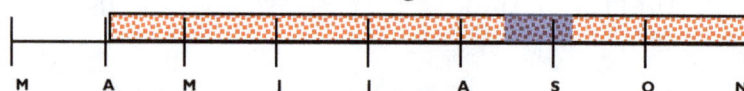

M	A	M	J	J	A	S	O	N

Host: Many herbaceous plants plus oak

Identification: This moth is typically red, with a prominent reniform spot and a smaller circular spot above the reniform. Usually there is a dark spot inside each end of the reniform spot.

9688 - *Galgula partita*
Wedgling Moth

M	A	M	J	J	A	S	O	N

Host: Wood sorrel

Identification: This moth is typically red, with dark shading between the reniform spot and the circular spot. There is also frequently a white spot where the post-medial line meets the margin of the forewing.

9669 - *Spodoptera ornithogalli*
Yellow-striped Armyworm Moth

9684 - *Elaphria grata*
Grateful Midget Moth

9688 - *Galgula partita*
Wedgling Moth

9689 - *Perigea xanthioides*
Red Groundling Moth

M	A	M	J	J	A	S	O	N

Host: Ironweed

Identification: This moth is easy to recognize with the red base color and yellow splotches and circles. There is also a series of black dots associated with the post-medial line.

9690 - *Condica videns*
White-dotted Groundling Moth

M	A	M	J	J	A	S	O	N

Host: Aster and goldenrod

Identification: This moth is poorly marked. Rely on the shiny forewings and white reniform spot for identification.

9930 - *Pyreferra citrombra*
Citrine Sallow Moth

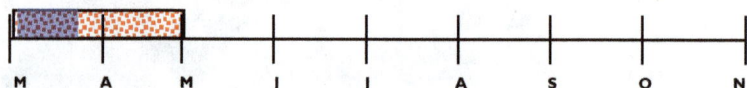

M	A	M	J	J	A	S	O	N

Host: unknown

Identification: This moth has three conspicuous lines on the forewings, with the outermost line making a 90 degree turn at the wing margin. Very little is known about this species.

9936 - *Eupsilia morrisoni*
Morrison's Sallow Moth

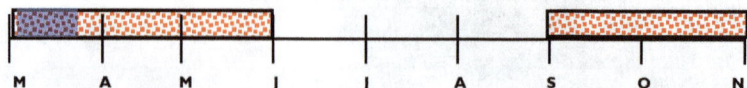

M	A	M	J	J	A	S	O	N

Host: Several deciduous tree species

Identification: This moth has two conspicuous lines on the forewings, with dark shading connecting the reniform spots.

9689 - *Perigea xanthioides*
Red Groundling Moth

9690 - *Condica videns*
White-dotted Groundling Moth

9930 - *Pyreferra citrombra*
Citrine Sallow Moth

9936 - *Eupsilia morrisoni*
Morrison's Sallow Moth

9944 - *Metaxaglaea viatica*
Roadside Sallow Moth

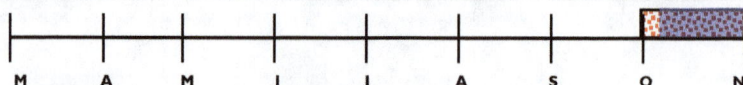

M A M J J A S O N

Host: Apple, crabapple, and cherry

Identification: This species has very prominent, white outlined reniform and orbicular spots, with the two actually touching or nearly so.

9952 - *Eucirroedia pampina*
Scalloped Sallow Moth

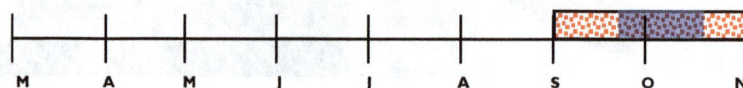

M A M J J A S O N

Host: Cherry and maple

Identification: Look for scalloping on the wings margins. Also, the reniform spot on this species is shaped like a dumbbell.

9957 - *Sunira bicolorago*
Bicolored Sallow Moth

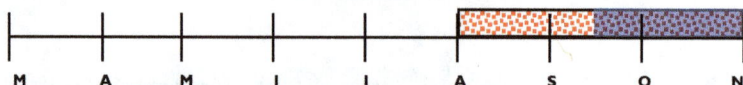

M A M J J A S O N

Host: A wide variety of plants

Identification: This moth has a variety of toothed and wavy lines, the prominence of which diminishes with age. The interior side of the reniform spot has a dark spot that persists with age.

9961 - *Anathix ralla*
Dotted Sallow Moth

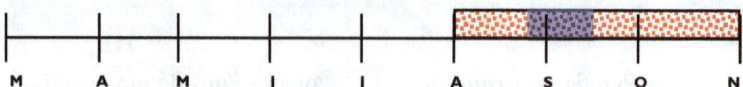

M A M J J A S O N

Host: Aspen

Identification: This moth is very similar to the Bicolored Sallow. One noticeable difference is the light colored veins in the forewing which penetrate through the dark post-medial band.

9944 - *Metaxaglaea viatica*
Roadside Sallow Moth

9952 – *Eucirroedia pampina*
Scalloped Sallow Moth

9957 - *Sunira bicolorago*
Bicolored Sallow Moth

9961 - *Anathix ralla*
Dotted Sallow Moth

10005 - *Feralia jocosa*
Joker Moth

M　A　M　J　J　A　S　O　N

Host: Hemlock and Pine

Identification: Look for the dark zigzag lines on the green base color. One of our earliest moths. Compare to other green Owlet Moths.

10008 - *Feralia comstocki*
Comstock's Sallow Moth

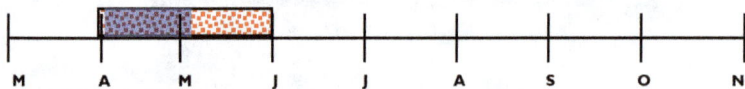

M　A　M　J　J　A　S　O　N

Host: Hemlock

Identification: This moth has the same black zigzag lines and green base color as The Joker. Comstock's differs in having dark patches on three sides of the reniform spot, whereas The Joker has but one dark patch.

10016 - *Psaphida styracis*
Fawn Sallow Moth

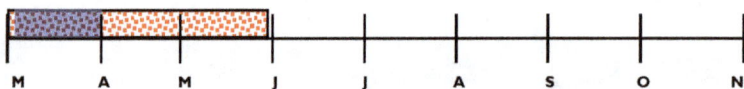

M　A　M　J　J　A　S　O　N

Host: Oak and ash

Identification: This is an extremely variable species with several color forms. The post-medial line usually runs parallel to the wing margin with the margin appearing frosted to some degree. The reniform spot is also paler in color in relation to the base color of the wing.

10005 – *Feralia jocose*
Joker Moth

10008 – *Feralia comstocki*
Comstock's Sallow Moth

10016 – *Psaphida styracis*
Fawn Sallow Moth

10020 - *Psaphida thaxterianus*
White-shouldered Sallow Moth

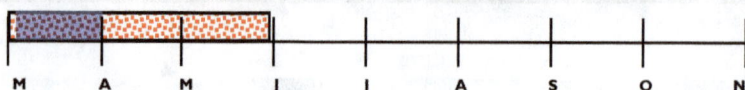

M   A   M   J   J   A   S   O   N

Host: White oak

Identification: Without a recognized common name, I have begun calling this moth the White-shouldered Sallow Moth due to the white patches prominently displayed near the forewing point of attachment. Very little is known about this moth.

10202 - *Cucullia convexipennis*
Brown-hooded Owlet Moth

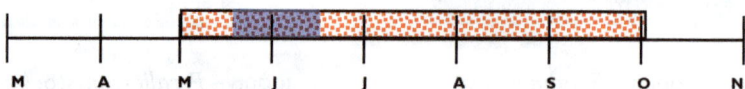

M   A   M   J   J   A   S   O   N

Host: Aster and goldenrod

Identification: There are but very few moths in our area with the wood-grain look. Notice that the wing tips are dark, the opposite of the Bicolored Woodgrain Moth (Hodge's #10520) that it might be confused with.

10288 - *Orthodes detracta*
Disparaged Arches Moth

M   A   M   J   J   A   S   O   N

Host: Several deciduous tree species including birch and oak

Identification: This moth is recognized by the pale reniform and orbicular spots in combination with rusty patches on the forewings.

10292 - *Melanchra adjuncta*
Hitched Arches Moth

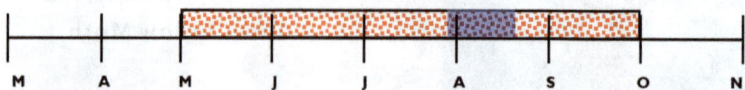

M   A   M   J   J   A   S   O   N

Host: A wide variety of plants

Identification: This moth has a pale spot at the base of the forewing along with the pale orbicular and reniform spots.

10020 – *Psaphida thaxterianus*
White-shouldered Sallow Moth

10202 – *Cucullia convexipennis*
Brown-hooded Owlet Moth

10288 - *Orthodes detracta*
Disparaged Arches Moth

10292 - *Melanchra adjuncta*
Hitched Arches Moth

10397 - *Lacinipolia renigera*
Bristly Cutworm Moth

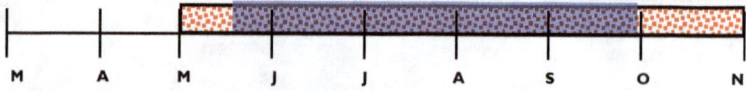

M	A	M	J	J	A	S	O	N

Host: Many herbaceous plants

Identification: Bristly Cutworm is easily recognized by the dark mask on the wings with green reniform spots.

10414 - *Lacinipolia implicata*
Implicit Arches

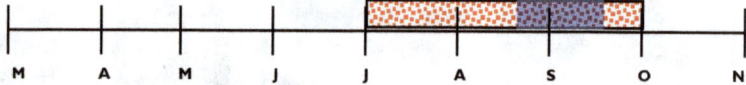

M	A	M	J	J	A	S	O	N

Host: Many herbaceous plants

Identification: Implicit Arches has a dark mask, unlike the other green Owlet Moths. The reniform spots are the same green color as the rest of the wing.

10438 - *Mythimna unipuncta*
Armyworm Moth

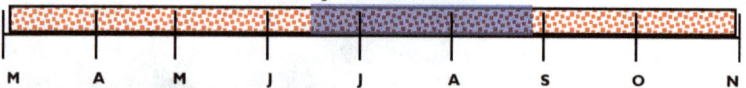

M	A	M	J	J	A	S	O	N

Host: A wide variety of plants

Identification: The white spot on the forewing is the key distinguishing feature of this species. Reniform and orbicular spots are usually very pale.

10445 - *Leucania linda*
Linda Wainscot Moth

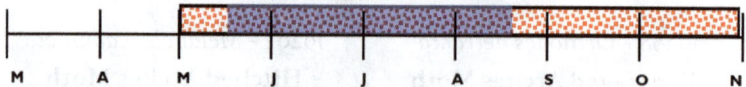

M	A	M	J	J	A	S	O	N

Host: Grasses

Identification: The prominent pale veins on the straw-colored background is unique among our moths.

10397 – *Lacinipolia renigera*
Bristly Cutworm Moth

10414 - *Lacinipolia implicata*
Implicit Arches

10438 - *Mythimna unipuncta*
Armyworm Moth

10445 – *Leucania linda*
Linda Wainscot Moth

10461 - *Leucania ursula*
Ursula Wainscot Moth

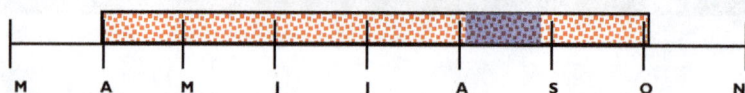

M	A	M	J	J	A	S	O	N

Host: Honeysuckle and crabgrass
Identification: This moth has the faint outline of a mask on the forewing, distinguishing it from Linda Wainscot.

10487 - *Orthosia rubescens*
Ruby Quaker Moth

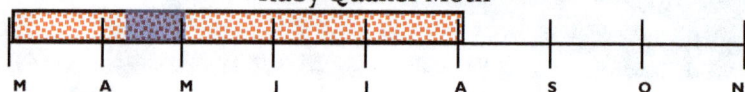

M	A	M	J	J	A	S	O	N

Host: Several deciduous trees species plus cattail
Identification: The reniform spot on this moth is colored-in dark on the interior side. The red wood-grain appearance of the forewings is unique.

10502 - *Himella fidelis*
Intractable Quaker Moth

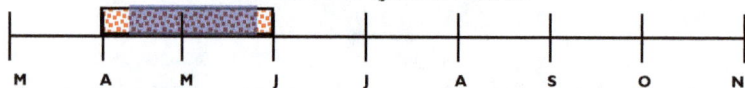

M	A	M	J	J	A	S	O	N

Host: Oak, elm, and crabapple
Identification: The orbicular and reniform spots as well as the post-medial line are all cream color. This species also has dark spots along the different lines. The moth pictured is quite worn.

10518 - *Achatia distincta*
Distinct Quaker Moth

M	A	M	J	J	A	S	O	N

Host: Several deciduous tree species
Identification: This moth is boldly marked. The dark 'frame' around the orbicular spot is consistent and obvious.

10461 - *Leucania ursula*
Ursula Wainscot Moth

10487 - *Orthosia rubescens*
Ruby Quaker Moth

10502 - *Himella fidelis*
Intractable Quaker Moth

10518 - *Achatia distincta*
Distinct Quaker Moth

10520 - *Morrisonia evicta*
Bicolored Woodgrain Moth

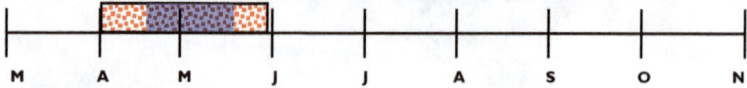

M A M J J A S O N

Host: Cherry

Identification: This another of our wood-grain Owlet Moths. Notice that the wing tips are light-colored in comparison to the Brown-hooded Owlet Moth. Also note the hook-like marking on the forewing (black arrow).

10663 - *Agrotis ipsilon*
Ipsilon Dart

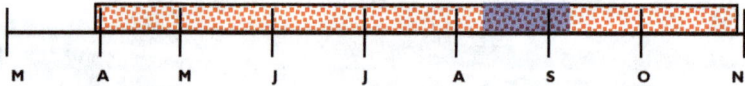

M A M J J A S O N

Host: Many cultivated plants

Identification: This moth is considered an agricultural pest and is found in nearly every state of the US. Two dark wedges on the forewing are key to identification, as one wedge extends down from the reniform spot, the other wedge up from the margin.

10670 - *Feltia jaculifera*
Dingy Cutworm Moth

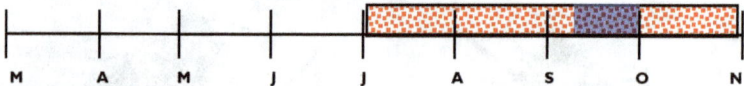

M A M J J A S O N

Host: Many herbaceous and cultivated plants

Identification: This species is also considered an agricultural pest. To distinguish this species from Subgothic Dart, look for the two prominent veins extending from the lower corner of the reniform spot.

10520 – *Morrisonia evicta*
Bicolored Woodgrain

10663 - *Agrotis ipsilon*
Ipsilon Dart

10670 - *Feltia jaculifera*
Dingy Cutworm Moth

10674 - *Feltia subgothica*
Subgothic Dart

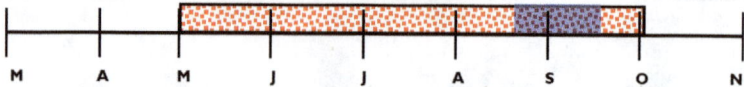

		M	J	J	A	S	O	N
M	A							

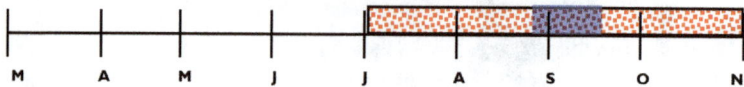

Host: Many herbaceous plants

Identification: The combination of light lines and dark 'fins' is very unique among our Butterfly Ridge moths.

10676 - *Feltia herilis*
Master's Dart

Host: Many herbaceous plants

Identification: This *Feltia* differs from the others by lacking a white line along the leading edge of the forewing and lacking two prominent veins extending from the corner of the reniform spot.

10891 - *Ochropleura implecta*
Flame-shouldered Dart

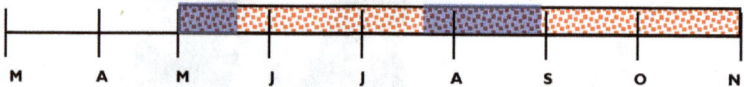

Host: Many herbaceous plants plus willow

Identification: The prominent cream-colored leading edge of the forewing is a unique feature of this moth. This species has two generations during the year.

10911 - *Anicla infecta*
Green Cutworm Moth

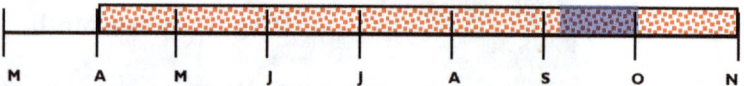

Host: Beets, tobacco, and grasses

Identification: Three dark spots within the reniform spot is unique to this species. Also note the darkening of the trailing edge of the forewing.

10674 - *Feltia subgothica*
Subgothic Dart

10676 - *Feltia herilis*
Master's Dart

10891 - *Ochropleura implecta*
Flame-shouldered Dart

10911 - *Anicla infecta*
Green Cutworm Moth

10942.1 - *Xestia dolosa*
Greater Black-letter Dart

| | | | | | | | |
|M|A|M|J|J|A|S|O|N|

Host: Clover, barley, and corn

Identification: The large arch just above the reniform spot is a good character to use to identify the Greater Black-letter Dart. Considered an agricultural pest. Nearly indistinguishable from Lesser Black-dart.

11003.1 - *Noctua pronuba*
Large Yellow Underwing Moth

| | | | | | | | |
|M|A|M|J|J|A|S|O|N|

Host: Agricultural crops

Identification: The hindwing is bright yellow with a single black band, however this moth is not a true Underwing (*Catocala*). The forewing features prominent orbicular and reniform spots as well as a pale forewing margin.

11029 - *Abagrotis alternata*
Greater Red Dart

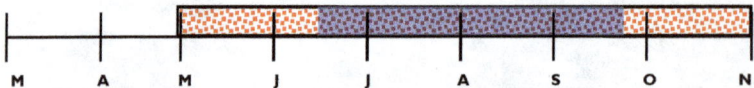

| | | | | | | | |
|M|A|M|J|J|A|S|O|N|

Host: Hickory, oak, walnut, and garden vegetables

Identification: The blood red markings on a straw-colored background is unique. Also look for the red reniform spot as well as a second red spot above the reniform spot.

10942.1 - *Xestia dolosa*
**Greater Black-letter
Dart Moth**

11003.1 - *Noctua pronuba*
**Large Yellow Underwing
Moth**

11029 – *Abagrotis
alternata*
**Greater Red Dart
Moth**

11068 - *Helicoverpa zea*
Corn Earworm Moth

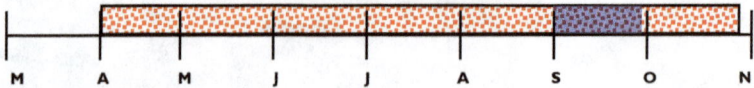

M A M J J A S O N

Host: Corn and other field crops

Identification: Perhaps the most distinctive characteristic for this non-descript moth is the hindwing, which is very pale with black veins and a dark patch at the bottom.

11128 - *Schinia arcigera*
Arcigera Flower Moth

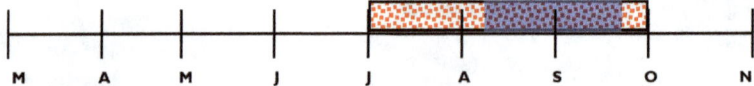

M A M J J A S O N

Host: Aster

Identification: The pale saddle on a chocolate brown background is very unique and sort of reminiscent of the Slug Moths. The legs of the Flower Moth however are not densely hairy like those of the Slug Moths.

11135 - *Schinia rivulosa*
Ragweed Flower Moth

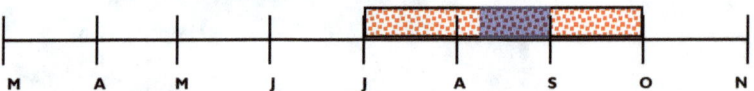

M A M J J A S O N

Host: Ragweed

Identification: The white lines on the Ragweed Flower Moth are much more prominent and undulating than that of the Arcigera Flower Moth. Otherwise, the two are very similar.

11068 – *Helicoverpa zea*
Corn Earworm Moth

11128 – *Schinia arcigera*
Arcigera Flower Moth

11135 - *Schinia rivulosa*
Ragweed Flower Moth

Index

Abagrotis alternata	322	Aethes argentilimitana	64
Acharia stimulea	78	Aglossa cuprina	100
Achatia distincta	316	Agonopterix	
Acleris		alstroemeriana	26
flavivittana	54	robinella	26
placidana	52	Agonopterix Moth,	
Acoloithus falsarius	66	Four-dotted	26
Acrobasis demotella	108	Agrotis ipsilon	318
Acrolophus		Agriphila vulgivagellus	96
arcanella	22	Allagrapha aerea	272
plumifrontella	22	Allotria elonympha	254
popeanella	22	Alypia octomaculata	296
Acronicta		Amorbia humerosana	64
afflicta	292	Amorpha juglandis	194
americana	286	Amphion floridensis	196
fallax	294	Anageshna primordialis	90
fragilis	290	Anagrapha falcifera	272
funeralis	288	Anathix ralla	308
hasta	288	Anavitrinella pampinaria	128
heitzmani	290	Ancylis	
increta	292	divisana	48
innotata	286	laciniana	48
interrupta	290	muricana	50
lithospila	294	Ancylis Moth,	
noctivaga	294	Red-headed	50
ovata	292	Two-toned	48
radcliffei	286	Angel Moth	170
spinigera	290	Angle Moth,	
tristis	292	Bicolored	122
vinnula	288	Blurry Chocolate	122
Actias luna	182	Common	122
Adaina ambrosiae	114	Faint-spotted	126
Adoneta spinuloides	76	Granite	124

Angle Moth, (cont'd)

Hemlock 124

Minor 122

Pale-marked 124

Promiscuous 48

Angle Shades Moth,

Brown 300

Anicla infecta 320

Anisota

stigma 178

virginiensis 178

Antaeotricha schlaegeri 28

Antepione thisoaria 150

Antheraea polyphemus 180

Apantesis

nais 222

phalerata 222

Apatelodes torrefacta 170

Apoda

biguttata 72

y-inversum 72

Appleworm Moth,

Many-dotted 302

Arches Moth,

Disparaged 312

Hitched 312

Implicit 314

Argyresthia oreasella 38

Argyrotaenia

alisellana 56

mariana 56

tabulana 56

velutinana 56

Armyworm Moth, 314

Yellow-striped 304

Artace cribrarius 172

Athetis tarda 302

Atroposia oenotherana 66

Atteva aurea 36

Autographa precationis 272

Automeris io 180

Badwing Moth 168

Balsa

malana 302

tristrigella 302

Balsa Moth,

Three-lined 302

Batman Moth 64

Battaristis vittella 34

Beautiful Eutelia Moth 274

Beauty Moth,

Oak 138

Pale 140

Tulip-tree 128

Beggar Moth 164

Bent-line Moth 50

Besma quercivoraria 146

Besma Moth,

Oak 146

Bird-dropping Moth,

Small 280

Tufted 280

Biston betularia 130

Black-bordered Lemon Moth 276

Black Zigzag Moth	282	Budworm Moth,	
Blepharomastix ranalis	90	Jack Pine	58
Blepharomastix Moth,			
Hollow-spotted	90	*Caenurgina erechtea*	256
Bleptina caradrinalis	234	*Callopistria floridensis*	302
Bold Medicine Moth	80	*Callosamia*	
Bomolocha Moth,		*angulifera*	184
Baltimore	240	*promethea*	182
Deceptive	242	*Caloptilia rhoifoliella*	24
Dimorphic	240	*Campaea perlata*	140
Flowing-line	240	*Caripeta*	
Gray-edged	242	*aretaria*	146
White-lined	242	*divisata*	146
Borer Moth,		*Carmenta bassiformis*	40
Cherry Shoot	38	Carpenterworm Moth	42
Deadwood	244	Carpet Moth,	
Indigo Stem	300	Bent-line	162
Locust Twig	52	Labrador	160
Loosestrife	160	Toothed Brown	162
Maple Callus	40	Unadorned	164
Northern Burdock	298	*Catocala*	
Sensitive Fern	298	*amatrix*	268
Waterlily	82	*andromedae*	268
White Pinecone	46	*angusi*	260
Broad-banded Eulogia Moth	110	*cerogama*	268
Brother Moth	284	*dejecta*	262
Brown Moth,		*epione*	258
Black-dotted	248	*flebilis*	260
White-spotted	92	*grynea*	270
Bucculatrix pomifoliella	24	*habilis*	258
Buck Moth	178	*ilia*	266
Budmoth,		*micronympha*	270
Tufted Apple	62		

Catocala (cont'd)

nebulosa	264
neogama	266
obscura	260
palaeogama	264
piatrix	258
residua	262
retecta	262
serena	260
subnata	264
ultronia	270
umbrosa	266
vidua	262
Cecropia Moth	184
Cenopis reticulatana	60
Ceratomia	
amyntor	188
catalpae	188
undulosa	188
Cerma cerintha	280
Chalcoela iphitalis	84
Chalceola Moth,	
Sooty-winged	84
Charadra deridens	284
Chimoptesis pennsylvaniana	48
Chionodes mediofuscella	34
Chionodes Moth,	
Black-smudged	34
Chlorochlamys chloroleucaria	154
Choristoneura	
fractivittana	58
parallela	58
pinus	58
rosaceana	58

Chrysendeton medicinalis	80
Chytolita morbidalis	234
Cisseps fulvicollis	226
Cissusa spadix	248
Cisthene	
packardii	214
plumbea	214
Citheronia	
regalis	174
sepulcralis	176
Cladara atroliturata	166
Cleora sublunaria	128
Clearwing Moth,	
Ironweed	40
Hummingbird	196
Snowberry	196
Clemensia albata	216
Clepsis peritana	60
Clostera albosigma	202
Clymene Moth	216
Cochylid Moth,	
Primrose	66
Coelostathma discopunctana	64
Coleophora	
mayrella	30
querciella	30
Coleophora Moth,	
Metallic	30
Colocasia	
flavicornis	284
propinquilinea	284
Common Eupithecia Moth	164
Common Oak Moth	246
Conchylodes ovulalis	94

Conchylodes Moth,
Zebra 94
Condica videns 306
Condylolomia participalis 102
Corn Earworm Moth 324
Corticivora clarki 50
Coryphista meadii 160
Cosmopterix dapifera 30
Costaconvexa centrostrigaria 162
Crambid Moth,
Rufous-banded 82
Crambidia uniformis 214
Crambus Moth,
Vagabond 96
Crocidophora tuberculalis 84
Crocidophora Moth,
Pale-winged 84
Cucullia convexipennis 312
Cutworm Moth,
Bristly 314
Dingy 318
Green 320
Cycnia tenera 224
Cyclophora packardi 156
Cydia
latiferreana 52
toreuta 50

Dagger Moth,
Afflicted 292
American 286
Delightful 288
Fragile 290

Dagger, (cont'd)
Funerary 288
Heitzman's 290
Interrupted 290
Night-wandering 294
Non-descript 290
Ovate 292
Radcliffe's 286
Southern Oak 292
Speared 288
Streaked 294
Unmarked 286
Darapsa
choerilus 200
myron 198
Dart Moth,
Flame-shouldered 320
Greater Black-letter 322
Greater Red 322
Ipsilon 318
Master's 320
Subgothic 320
Dasychira vagans 228
Dasylophia
anguina 208
thyatiroides 210
Datana sp. 202
Deidamia inscriptum 198
Delicate Cycnia Moth 224
Desmia funeralis 88
Devil Moth,
Little 36
Pine 176

331

Diacme adipaloides	86	Emerald Moth,	
Diacme Moth,		Red-fringed	152
Darker	86	Showy	152
Diasemiodes janassialis	88	Wavy-lined	154
Diastictis ventralis	92	White-fringed	152
Diathrausta harlequinalis	88	*Emmelina monodactyla*	116
Dichomeris		*Ennomos magnaria*	140
flavocostella	34	*Ephestiodes infimella*	110
nonstrigella	36	*Epicallima argenticinctella*	28
Dichomeris Moth,		Epicallima Moth,	
Cream-edged	34	Orange-headed	28
Dichorda iridaria	152	*Epimecis hortaria*	128
Dichrorampha bittana	50	*Epipaschia superatalis*	104
Digrammia ocellinata	126	Esther Moth	132
Dioryctria resinosella	110	*Eubaphe mendica*	164
Dimorphic Tosale Moth	102	*Euchaetes egle*	226
Dolichomia Moth,		*Euchlaena*	
Pink-fringed	100	*amoenaria*	136
Dot-lined White Moth	172	*obtusaria*	134
Dotted Ecdytolopha Moth	52	*pectinaria*	136
Drab Condylolomia Moth	102	*tigrinaria*	136
Drepana arcuata	118	Euchlaena Moth,	
Dryocampa rubicunda	176	Deep Yellow	136
Dyspteris abortivaria	168	Forked	136
		Mottled	136
Eacles imperialis	174	Obtuse	134
Eastern Panthea Moth	282	*Eucirroedia pampina*	308
Ecdytolopha insiticiana	52	*Euclea delphinii*	76
Ectropis crepuscularia	128	*Eucosma*	
Elaphria grata	304	*ochroterminana*	46
Ellida caniplaga	206	*parmatana*	46
Elophila gyralis	82	*raracana*	46
		tocullionana	46

Eucosma Moth,
Aster 46
Eudonia strigalis 80
Eudonia Moth,
Striped 80
Eudryas grata 296
Eufidonia notaria 130
Eugonobapta nivosaria 64
Eulithis diversilineata 158
Eulogia ochrifrontella 110
Eumarozia malachitana 44
Eumorpha pandorus 194
Euparthenos nubilis 254
Eupithecia
absenthiata 166
miserulata 164
palpata 164
• Eupsilia morrisoni 306
Eusarca confusaria 148
Eusarca Moth,
Confused 148
Eutelia pulcherrimus 274
Euthyatira pudens 118
Eutrapela clemataria 148
Exoteleia pinifoliella 32

Fascista cercerisella 34
Feltia
heralis 320
jaculifera 318
subgothica 320

Feralia
jocosa 310
majot 310
Ferguson's Scallop Shell Moth 160
Fern Moth,
Florida 302
Filbertworm Moth 52
Filigreed Moth 48
Flannel Moth,
Black-waved 68
White 68
Flower Moth,
Arcigera 324
Ragweed 324
Forester Moth,
Eight-spotted 296
Fruitworm Moth,
Reticulated 60
Schlaeger's 28
Fulgoraecia exigua 78
Fungus Moth,
Common 244
Furcula
borealis 208
cinereal 208
Furcula Moth,
Gray 208
White 208

Galasa nigrinodis 102
Galgula partita 304

Gandaritis atricolorata   160
Geina
   buscki   114
   periscelidactylus   114
Gem Moth   162
Geometer Moth,
   Barberry   160
   Chickweed   158
   Crocus   138
   Curve-toothed   148
   Dark-banded   160
   False Crocus   138
   Kent's   140
   Snowy   64
   Yellow-veined   126
Giant Leopard Moth   220
Glaphyria glaphyralis   82
Glaphyria Moth,
   Common   82
Gluphisia septentrionis   206
Gluphisia Moth,
   Common   206
Granite Moth   48
Grapevine Epimenis Moth   296
Grass Moth,
   Spotted   238
Grass-veneer Moth,
   Double-banded   96
   Elegant   96
   Gold-stripe   96
   Graceful   98

Gray Moth,
   Bent-line   126
   Brown-shade   126
   Common   128
   Double-lined   128
Grease Moth   100
Green Cloverworm Moth   242
Green Marvel Moth   294
Groundling Moth,
   Red   306
   White-dotted   306
Gymnandrosoma punctidiscanum   52

Haematopis grataria   158
Hag Moth   30
Halysidota tessellaris   224
Haploa
   clymene   216
   lecontei   218
Haploa Moth,
   Leconte's   218
Harpetogramma sphingealis   38
Harrisina americana   66
Hayworm Moth,
   Clover   100
Hellinsia
   lacteodactylus   116
   unicolor   116
Helicoverpa zea   324
Heliomata cycladata   120
Hemaris
   diffinis   196
   thysbe   196

Hemileuca maia	178	Hypena, (cont'd)		
Herpetogramma		madefactalis	242
abdominalis	92	manalis	242
aeglealis	94	scabra	240
sphingealis	94	Hypercompe scribonia	242
thestealis	94	Hyphantria cunea	220
Herpetogramma Moth,		Hypoprepia	220
Zigzag	94	fucosa	216
Heterocampa Moth,		miniata	216
Oblique	210	Hypsopygia	
White-blotched	210	binodulalis	100
Heterocampa		costalis	100
obliqua	210	Hypsoropha hormos	246
umbrata	210		
Heterophleps triguttaria	166	Idaea scintillularia	156
Himella fidelis	316	Idia	
Holomelina Moth,		aemula	230
Immacualte	218	americalis	230
Homadaula anisocentra	36	lubricalis	232
Hooktip Moth,		rotundalis	230
Arched	118	Idia Moth,	
Hyalophora cecropia	184	American	230
Hydrelia inornata	164	Common	230
Hyles lineata	200	Glossy Black	232
Hymenia perspectalis	88	Rotund	230
Hypagyrtis		Imperial Moth	174
esther	132	Io Moth	180
unipunctata	132	Iridopsis	
Hypena		defectaria	126
abalienalis	242	larvaria	126
baltimoralis	242	Isa textual	76
bijugalis	240	Isochaetes beutenmuelleri	74
deceptalis	240		

Joker Moth 310

Labyrinth Moth 44
Lacinipolia
  implicata 314
  renigera 314
Lacosoma chiridota 168
Lagoa crispata 68
Lambdina fervidaria 146
Lapara coniferarum 190
Lappet Moth 172
Large Lace-border Moth 158
Laugher Moth 284
Leaffolder Moth,
  Grape 88
  Redbud 34
Leafroller Moth,
  Basswood 92
  Black-spotted 42
  Broken-banded 58
  Gray 60
  Gray-banded 56
  Locust 108
  Multiform 54
  Oblique-banded 58
  Parallel-banded 58
  Red-banded 56
  Three-lined 54
  White-line 64
  White-spotted 56
  Woodgrain 54

Leaftier Moth
  Boxwood 102
  Celery 86
  Tulip-tree 42
Leconte's Haploa 112
Leucania
  linda 314
  ursula 316
Leuconycta
  diphteroides 280
  lepidula 280
Leuconycta Moth,
  Green 280
  Marbled-green 280
Lichen Moth,
  Lead-colored 214
  Little White 216
  Packard's 214
  Painted 216
  Scarlet-winged 216
  Uniform 214
Lithacodes fasciola 70
Lithacodia musta 278
Lithacodia Moth,
  Black-dotted 278
  Large Mossy 278
  Pink-barred 278
  Small Mossy 278
Lochmaeus bilineata 212
Lomographa vestaliata 134

Looper Moth,
Blackberry 154
Celery 272
Clover 138
Common 272
Curve-lined 146
Forage 256
Lesser Grapevine 158
Gray Spruce 146
Maple 254
Pine False 250
Small Pine 164
Southern Pine 146
Unspotted 272
Lophocampa caryae 224
Lophosis labeculata 158
Lucerne Moth 86
Luna Moth 182

Macalla Moth,
Dimorphic 104
Macaria
aemulataria 122
bicolorata 122
fissinotata 124
granitata 124
minorata 122
promiscuata 122
signaria 124
transitaria 122
Macramé Moth 44
Malacosoma disstria 174
Maliattha synochitis 278

Manduca
jasminearum 186
sexta 186
Marathyssa inficita 274
Marathyssa Moth,
Dark 274
Marimatha nigrofimbria 276
Meganola
minuscula 276
phylla 276
Meganola Moth,
Coastal Plain 276
Confused 276
Melanchra adjuncta 312
Melanolophia canadaria 130
Melanolophia Moth,
Canadian 130
Mellilla xanthometata 120
Meropleon diversicolor 298
Metalectra discalis 244
Metarranthis
angularia 140
homuraria 142
Metarranthis Moth,
Angled 140
Purplish 142
Metaxaglaea viatica 308
Microcrambus
biguttellus 96
elegans 96
Midget Moth,
Grateful 304
Mimoschinia rufofascialis 82

Miner Moth,
  Sumac Leafblotch 24
Misogada unicolor 210
Mocis texana 256
Mocis Moth,
  Texas 256
Morrisonia evicta 318
Mythimna unipuncta 314

Nadata gibbosa 202
Natada nasoni 74
Necklace Moth,
  Small 246
Needleminer Moth,
  Pine 32
Nemoria
  bistriaria 152
  mimosaria 152
Neoligia crytora 298
Nerice bidentata 206
Nigetia formosalis 238
Noctua pronuba 322
Nomophila nearctica 86
Norape ovina 68

Oakworm Moth,
  Pink-striped 178
  Spiny 178
Ochropleura implecta 320
Odontosia elegans 206
Olceclostera angelica 170
Oligocentria semirufescens 212
One-spotted Variant Moth 132

Oneida lunulalis 104
Orange-tufted Oneida Moth 104
Orangewing Moth 120
Orgyia leucostigma 228
Orthodes detracta 312
Orthofidonia flavivenata 126
Orthonama obstipata 162
Orthosia rubescens 316
Oruza albocostaliata 276
Owlet Moth,
  Bent-winged 234
  Brown-hooded 312
  Curve-lined 244
  Decorated 244
  Morbid 234
  Thin-winged 238

Pachysphinx modesta 194
Packardia geminata 70
Packard's Concealer Moth 28
Paectes
  oculatrix 274
  pygmaea 274
Paectes Moth,
  Eyed 274
  Pygmy 274
Palpita
  illibalis 90
  magniferalis 90
Palpita Moth,
  Inkblot 90
  Splendid 90

Palthis		*Parasa chloris*	76
angulalis	236	*Pasiphila rectangulata*	166
asopialis	236	*Peoria approximella*	112
Palthis Moth,		Peppered Moth	130
Dark-spotted	236	*Peridea*	
Faint-spotted	236	*angulosa*	204
Pandemis		*basitriens*	204
lamprosana	54	*ferruginea*	204
limitata	54	*Perigea xanthioides*	306
Pangrapta decoralis	244	*Pero ancetaria*	138
Panopoda		Pero Moth,	
carneicosta	246	Hubner's	138
rufimargo	246	*Phaecasiophora*	
Panopoda Moth,		*confixana*	44
Brown	246	*niveiguttana*	44
Red-lined	246	*Phaeoura quernaria*	138
Panthea		*Phalonidia lepidana*	64
acronyctoides	282	Phaneta Moth,	
furcilla	282	Buff-tipped	46
Pantographa limata	92	Reddish	46
Paonias		*Pheosia rimosa*	204
astylus	192	*Phigalia denticulate*	134
excaecata	192	Phigalia Moth,	
myops	192	Toothed	134
Papaipema		*Phlogophora periculosa*	300
arctivorens	298	*Phoberia atomaris*	246
baptisiae	300	*Phobetron pithecium*	74
inquaesita	298	*Phosphila turbulenta*	300
Parallelia bistriaris	254	Phosphila Moth,	
Paralobesia liriodendrana	42	Turbulent	300
Parapediasia		*Phyllodesma americana*	172
decorellus	98	*Phyprosopus callitrichoides*	244
teterrella	98	Pink-fringed Dolichomia	40

Plagodis
 alcoolaria 144
 fervidaria 144
 kuetzingi 144
 phlogosaria 144
 pulveraria 142
 serinaria 144
Plagodis Moth,
 Fervid 144
 Hollow-spotted 144
 Lemon 144
 Purple 144
 Straight-line 144
Planthopper Parasite Moth 78
Platynota
 exasperatana 62
 flavedana 62
 idaeusalis 62
Platynota Moth,
 Black-shaded 62
 Exasperating 62
Platyptilia carduidactylus 114
Pleuroprucha insulsaria 156
Plume Moth,
 Ambrosia 114
 Artichoke 114
 Grape 114
 Morning-glory 116
Pococera
 asperatella 106
 expandens 106
 maritimalis 106
 militella 106
 robustella 104

Polygrammodes flavidalis 92
Poison Hemlock Moth 26
Polygrammate hebraeicum 296
Polyphemus Moth 180
Ponometia erastrioides 280
Powder Moth 130
Prionoxystus robiniae 42
Probole amicaria 142
Probole Moth,
 Friendly 142
Prochoerodes transversata 150
Prolimacodes badia 72
Promethea Moth 182
Prominent Moth,
 Angulose 204
 Black-rimmed 204
 Black-spotted 208
 Chocolate 204
 Double-lined 212
 Double-toothed 206
 Drab 210
 Elegant 206
 Gray-patched 210
 Linden 206
 Morning-glory 212
 Oval-based 204
 Red-washed 212
 Sigmoid 202
 White-dotted 202
 White-headed 106
Protoboarmia porcelaria 50
Protodeltote muscosula 278
Psaphida
 styracis 310
 thaxterianus 312

Pseudeustrotia carneola 278
Pseudochelaria
  pennsylvanica 32
  walsinghami 32
Pseudothyatira cymatophoroides 118
Psycholorpha epimenis 296
Pug Moth,
  Green 166
Pyrausta
  acrionalis 84
  bicoloralis 84
  niveicilialis 86
Pyrausta Moth,
  Bicolored 84
  Mint-loving 84
  White-fringed 86
Pyreferra citrombra 306
Pyromorpha dimidiata 68
Pyrrharctia isabella 218

Quaker Moth,
  Distinct 316
  Intractable 316
  Ruby 316

Raphia frater 284
Reddish Ephestiodes Moth 110
Redectis vitrea 238
Redectis Moth,
  White-spotted 238
Regal Moth 174
Renia discoloralis 236
Renia Moth,
  Discolored 236

Retinia gemistrigulana 44
Rheumaptera prunivorata 160
Rivula propinqualis 238
Root Moth,
  Ironweed 92
  Rosy Maple Moth 176

Sack-bearer Moth,
  Scalloped 168
Saddleback Caterpillar Moth 78
Salebriaria rufimacalatella 108
Salebriaria Moth,
  White-banded 108
Sallow Moth,
  Bicolored 308
  Citrine 306
  Dotted 308
  Fawn 310
  Major 310
  Morrison's 306
  Roadside 308
  Scalloped 308
  White-shouldered 312
Schinia
  arcigera 324
  rivulosa 324
Schizura
  ipomaea 212
  leptinoides 212
Schizura Moth,
  Black-blotched 212
Schreckensteinia erythriella 38

Sciota		
subcaesiella	108	
vetustella	108	
Scolecocampa liburna	244	
Scoparia biplagialis	80	
Scoparia Moth,		
Double-striped	80	
Scopula limboundata	158	
Scribbler Moth	166	
Sculptured Moth	44	
Sedgeminer Moth,		
Multicolored	298	
Seedworm Moth,		
Eastern Pine	50	
Selenia kentaria	140	
Semioscopis packardella	28	
Shoot Moth,		
Red Pine	110	
Walnut	108	
Sinoe robiniella	32	
Skeletonizer Moth,		
Apple	24	
Clemens' False	66	
Grapeleaf	66	
Skiff Moth	72	
Slant-line Moth,		
White	148	
Yellow	148	
Slowpoke Moth	302	
Slug Moth,		
Abbreviated Button	70	
Crowned	76	
Jeweled Tailed	70	

Slug Moth, (cont'd)		
Monkey	74	
Nason's	74	
Purple-crested	76	
Red-crossed Button	70	
Shagreened	72	
Spiny-oak	76	
Spun Glass	74	
Yellow-collared	72	
Yellow-shouldered	70	
Small Engrailed Moth	128	
Smaller Parasa Moth	76	
Smoky Moth,		
Orange-patched	68	
Snout Moth,		
Carmine	112	
Spanworm Moth,		
Large Maple	150	
Lesser Maple	120	
Maple	140	
Sparganothis tristriata	60	
Sparganothis Moth,		
Three-streaked	60	
Speranza pustularia	120	
Sphecodina abbottii	198	
Sphinx kalmiae	190	
Sphinx Moth,		
Abbott's	198	
Ash	186	
Azalea	200	
Big Poplar	194	
Blind-eyed	192	
Carolina	186	

Sphinx Moth, (cont'd)

Catalpa	188
Elm	188
Huckleberry	192
Laurel	190
Lettered	198
Nessus	196
Pandorus	194
Small-eyed	192
Southern Pine	190
Tersa	200
Virginia Creeper	198
Walnut	194
Waved	188
White-lined	200

Spilosoma congrua	218
Spodoptera ornithogalli	304
Spotted Apatelodes Moth	170
Spragueia leo	282

Spragueia Moth,

Common	282

Spring Moth,

Common	120
White	134
Stained Lophosis Moth	158
Stripe-backed Moth	34
Sunira bicolorago	308
Swammerdamia caesiella	38
Symmerista Moth	208
Symmerista sp.	208
Synanthedon acerni	40
Synchlora aerate	154
Syndemis afflictana	60

Tent Caterpillar Moth,

Forest	174

Tetracis

cachexiata	148
crocallata	148
The Hebrew	296
Theisoa constrictella	30
Three-spotted Fillip Moth	166

Thyatirid Moth,

Dogwood	118
Tufted	118
Thyris maculata	112

Thyris Moth,

Spotted	112

Tiger Moth,

Agreeable	218
Harnessed	222
Isabella	218
Nais	222
Tolype velleda	172

Tolype Moth,

Large	172

Tortricidia

flexuosa	70
pallida	70

Tortrix Moth,

Garden	60
Tosale oviplagalis	102

Tube Moth,

Jack Pine	56

Tubeworm Moth,

Clemen's Grass	22
Eastern Grass	22
Grass	22

Tulip-tree Silkmoth	184	Underwing Moth, (cont'd)	
Tussock Moth,		Ultronia	270
Banded	224	Umber	266
Hickory	224	Widow	262
Milkweed	226	Woody	270
Variable	228	Yellow-banded	268
White-marked	228	Yellow-gray	262
Twin-spot Moth,		Youthful	264
Red	162	*Urola nivalis*	98
Udea rubigalis	86	Urola Moth,	
Umber Moth		Snowy	98
American Barred	142		
Underwing Moth,		Variable Antepione Moth	150
Andromeda	268	*Varneria postremella*	110
Angus'	260	*Virbia immaculata*	218
Bride	266		
Clouded	264	Wainscot Moth,	
Dejected	262	Linda	314
Epione	258	Ursula	316
False	254	Wave Moth,	
Habilis	258	Common Tan	156
Ilia	266	Diminutive	156
Large Yellow	322	Packard's	156
Little Nymph	270	Webworm Moth,	
Locust	254	Ailanthus	36
Mournful	260	Bluegrass	98
Obscure	260	Fall	220
Old-wife	264	Harlequin	88
Penitent	258	Maple	106
Residua	262	Mimosa	36
Serene	260	Pine	104
Sweetheart	268	Serpentine	94

Spotted Beet	88	*Zale, (cont'd)*	
Striped Oak	106	*squamularis*	250
Sycamore	106	*undularis*	248
Yellow-spotted	90	*unilineata*	252
Wedgling Moth	304	Zale Moth,	
White Edge Moth	276	Black	248
Wood Nymph,		Colorful	250
Beautiful	296	Gray-banded	250
Woodgrain Moth,		Horrid	252
Bicolored	318	Intent	252
		Lunate	248
Xanthorhoe		One-lined	252
ferrugata	162	Washed-out	252
labradorensis	160	*Zanclognatha*	
lacustrata	162	*jacchusalis*	234
Xanthotype		*laevigata*	232
sospeta	138	*Zanclognatha (cont'd)*	
urticaria	138	*lituralis*	232
Xestia dolosa	322	*obscuripennis*	234
Xylophanes tersa	200	Zanclognatha Moth,	
		Dark	234
Yellow-collared Scape Moth	226	Lettered	232
Yellowhorn Moth,	284	Variable	232
Close-banded	284	Wavy-lined	234

Zale	
duplicata	250
horrida	252
intenta	252
lunata	248
metatoides	252
minerea	250
phaeocapna	250

Notes

Notes

Notes

Notes

Notes

Notes

Notes

www.ingramcontent.com/pod-product-compliance
Lightning Source LLC
Chambersburg PA
CBHW060307030426
42336CB00011B/963